THE KOSHER COMPANION

THE KOSHER COMPANION

A Guide to Food, Cooking, Shopping, and Services

Trudy Garfunkel

A Birch Lane Press Book
Published by Carol Publishing Group

A Birch Lane Press Book
Published by Carol Publishing Group
Birch Lane Press is a registered trademark of Carol Communications, Inc.

Editorial, sales and distribution, rights and permission inquiries should be addressed to: Carol Publishing Group, 120 Enterprise Avenue, Secaucus, N.J. 07094

In Canada: Canadian Manda Group, One Atlantic Avenue, Suite 105, Toronto, Ontario M6K 3E7

Carol Publishing Group books may be purchased in bulk at special discounts for sales promotion, fund-raising, or educational purposes. Special editions can be created to specifications. For details, contact: Special Sales Department, Carol Publishing Group, 120 Enterprise Avenue, Secaucus, N.J. 07094

Designed by Andrew B. Gardner

Manufactured in the United States of America
10   9   8   7   6   5   4   3   2   1

Library of Congress Cataloging-in-Publication Data

Garfunkel, Trudy.
    The kosher companion : a guide to food, cooking, shopping, and services / Trudy Garfunkel.
       p.   cm.
    ISBN 1-55972-397-1
    1. Cookery, Jewish.   2. Kosher food.   I. Title.
TX 724.G37   1997
641.5'676—DC21   97-389
                                                                         CIP

CONTENTS

> **kosher** Kosher adj. Honest; authentic; valid; ethical; ful-
> filling the minimum requirements of honesty or ethics.
> From "kosher" = clean and acceptable, according to
> Jewish dietary laws. Word taken from Hebrew to Yiddish
> to English.
>
> —*The Dictionary of American Slang*

You don't have to be Jewish to buy and eat kosher food. In fact, only 25 percent of the consumers who purchase kosher food in the United States are Jews. In the past few years, kosher has become one of the fastest-growing trends in the food industry. Publications as diverse as *Adweek, Food and Wine Magazine,* and *Rolling Stone* have declared kosher to be one of the hot food trends of the nineties. Tens of thousands of U.S. packaged goods are already certified kosher, and a thousand new products are added to the list each year. Integrated Marketing Communications, which sponsors an international kosher foods and food services trade show each year, estimates that by the year 2000 there will be fifty thousand kosher certified products available.

Kosher is big business. According to *Gourmet News,* the dollar value of the kosher market in America is $3 billion a year. The dollar value spent on all kosher certified products—whether or not they were purchased specifically because they were kosher—is $35 billion. Over 8,100 companies—including such giants as Procter & Gamble, Pillsbury, Kraft, Coca-Cola, General

Mills, Hershey, Nabisco, Heinz, and Dannon—have spent time, effort, and money to earn the coveted kosher certification.

Why has kosher become so popular? There are a number of reasons. In recent years there has been a resurgence of people going back to their Jewish roots and becoming more observant of kosher laws. There are also other groups who purchase kosher foods to meet their religious beliefs. These include 5.5 million American Muslims who follow dietary laws similar to those of Orthodox Jews, and the 800,000 American Seventh-Day Adventists, who are encouraged to follow the dietary guidelines given in the Bible—the basis of kosher.

Another reason for the burgeoning kosher market is the growing number of health-conscious consumers who believe that since kosher certification is given by independent, non-governmental agencies (and certification has its own strict labeling laws and stringent meat and poultry inspection), it represents a kind of extra "Good Housekeeping seal of approval." For them, buying and eating kosher means healthier, safer food. Then there are the millions of Americans who are vegetarians. And the 1 to 2 percent of the American population who suffer from a variety of allergies or food intolerances: people who are allergic to shellfish or milk, for example, and who, like vegetarians, must know exactly what ingredients are in the processed foods they buy.

The Kosher Companion is a consumer's guide to the ever-growing world of kosher food and kosher products. It explains the meaning of kosher and how to identify the variety of symbols used to designate kosher products. There are chapters on buying kosher meats and poultry, and on identifying kosher products for vegetarians and those who are lactose-intolerant or allergic to milk. There are tips on how to buy foods that are both healthy and kosher, including a selection of easy-to-prepare kosher recipes from the kitchens of my family and friends, as well as information on kosher wines, buying kosher products by mail, and where to find kosher hotels, restaurants, supermarkets, and caterers.

GLOSSARY

Bodek The trained inspector who looks for abnormalities in a slaughtered animal's lungs and other organs.

Fleishig (sometimes Fleishedik) Yiddish for kosher meat, including poultry. Also used to refer to meat dishes and utensils.

Hechsher The symbol that indicates kosher certification.

Kashering/Koshering The act of making something kosher; the process by which utensils and equipment are made fit for kosher use.

Kashrut (kashrus, kashruth) Term related to aspects of food preparation according to Jewish laws; the complete written code of religious dietary laws governing every single act of eating.

Kosher Term used to describe foods that meet the requirements of the Jewish dietary laws.

Mashgiah A kosher investigator or supervisor.

Milchig (sometimes Milchedik) Yiddish for dairy products. Also refers to dairy dishes, utensils, and equipment.

Pareve Neutral foods containing neither dairy nor meat ingredients.

Shehitah   The conditions that meat and poultry must satisfy in order to be considered kosher; the process of ritual slaughter of meat and poultry.

Shohet   A ritual slaughterer.

Talmud   The massive encyclopedia of Jewish thought and commentary compiled in the first few centuries C.E.

Torah   The first five books of the Bible; the Five Books of Moses and the oral law which were given to the Israelites on Mount Sinai.

Trayf   Food that is unfit or improper to eat according to Jewish dietary laws.

CHAPTER ONE

WHAT IS KOSHER?

Kosher is the anglicized version of the Hebrew word *kasher*, meaning "fit" or "proper to be used." Food is kosher when its ingredients and the means of its manufacture have adhered to a certain set of stringent and demanding laws and restrictions. You can't make foods kosher just by saying prayers over them. Nor does it have the same meaning as "kosher style," a phrase used to describe certain ethnic dishes or food preparations (such as "kosher" dill pickles or "kosher style" delicatessen) or foods derived from Eastern European Jewish cuisines.

Kosher means adherence to the Jewish dietary laws—some nearly 3,500 years old—that have their origins in passages of the Torah (the first five books of the Bible: Genesis, Exodus, Leviticus, Numbers, Deuteronomy). These were later elaborated on by rabbis who, in the Talmud, added further requirements and restrictions. (Hebrew for "study," the Talmud is the massive encyclopedia of Jewish thought, commentary, and civil and religious law compiled in the first few centuries C.E.) The word *kosher* itself does not appear in the five books of Moses, although it can be found a few times in later books of the Bible. But even here it does not refer to food specifically, but to the "fitness" of items used in religious rituals.

The kosher dietary laws and rules, known as kashrut (also spelled kashrus or kashruth), govern many aspects of food preparation, cooking, and consumption for observant Jews. They include instructions for the ritual slaughter of ani-

1

mals, which foods are permitted, and which are prohibited. Although the purpose of these laws may have had a positive effect on health (see chapter 6), their original purpose was religious, an act of devotion and affirmation of faith that expressed spiritual and moral values. They provided a diet for the soul as well as for the body. The dietary laws imposed a type of self-discipline on one of the most basic elements of life—eating.

In Jewish teaching, eating is regarded as a hallowed act. The twentieth-century religious philosopher Martin Buber (1878–1965) wrote that kashrut hallowed the everyday by turning a natural function, eating, into something holy. Kashrut also teaches a reverence for all life. There are many admonitions in the Torah forbidding cruelty to animals, including the mandate not to "cause pain to any living creature." The Torah preaches compassion and respect for all living things, going so far as to prohibit eating animals killed by hunters, adding that animals should not be killed for anything other than food or self-preservation.

Some of the dietary laws are stated clearly in the Bible; others took on interpreted meanings through the writings and commentaries of generations of Talmudic rabbis. No explicit reasons are given in the Bible for many of the prohibitions and mandates in the dietary laws. Decreed by God, they are considered divine directives that need no rationale or explanation other than that following them leads to holiness. (The Hebrew word for holiness is *kedushah*, which is derived from the word *kodesh*, meaning separateness.)

As *The Jewish Book of Why*, by Alfred J. Kolatch, explains, "Whatever was holy was something apart, to be set aside. To be a holy people, Israel had to be apart, separated from their idol-worshipping neighbors. The dietary laws were instituted as one means of making the Jewish lifestyle different from that of their neighbors." Through the ages, the dietary laws have helped define Jewish life, giving the Jewish people a cohesive yet distinct identity.

The basic details of the dietary laws include:

❧ *A prohibition against mixing meat and milk:*
"You shall not seethe a kid in its mother's milk," Exod. 23:19; also Exod. 34:26 and Deut. 14:21. This commandment, which is mentioned three times, led to the rule against cooking or consuming meat and milk or dairy products together at one meal.

As with other dietary laws, the Bible offers no reason for this prohibition, although scholars think it may have derived from an abhorrence of pagan practices or rituals, or as an extension of the commandment against cruelty to animals. For what could be more indifferent or cruel than first to kill an animal and then mix its flesh with the liquid that gave it life?

❧ *A prohibition against the consumption of blood:*
"You shall eat no manner of blood, whether of fowl or beast"; "The life of all flesh is the blood thereof," Lev. 17:14. There are numerous mentions in the Bible of blood as the symbol of the essence of humankind. In Judaism, eating or drinking of blood is considered a desecration of life itself. This belief led to a key element of kosher food preparation—the removal of blood from meat. The early rabbis concluded that when animals are killed for food, care should be taken to remove or drain as much blood as possible before the meat is cooked.

❧ *A list of permitted animals:*
"Of the animals you may eat any that hath both true cloven hooves and that brings up its cud," Lev. 11:3; "Among the mammals that you may eat are the ox, the goat, the gazelle, the deer, the antelope, the ibex, the chamois, the bison, and the giraffe," Deut. 14:4; "You may eat any creature that lives in salt water or fresh water, as long as it has fins and scales," Lev. 11:9; "Of all the pure birds you may eat" (twenty-four forbidden species of fowl are then listed), Deut. 14:11.

❧ *A prohibition against eating certain animals:*
"All creatures in seas and rivers that have no fins and scales, whether invertebrates or mammals or other creatures, are an abomination to you," Lev. 11:10; "These are the smaller animals that breed on land which are unclean to you" (a list of rodents, reptiles, and mollusks follows), Lev. 1:29; "All the winged swarming things are unclean to you; they shall not be eaten," Deut. 14:19.

Again, no reasons are given in the Bible as to why some fish and animals are proper to eat and others are forbidden. However, the identifying characteristics that make a creature fit for consumption are provided: mammals must both chew their cud and have a split or cloven hoof; fish must have both fins and scales that are removable without damaging or tearing the skin. The characteristics of permitted birds are not listed; only prohibited birds are named, such as birds of prey. Later traditions, however, allowed that domestic fowl and birds that have a projecting claw, a crop, and a gizzard or stomach whose inner lining can readily be peeled were kosher.

❧ *The ritual slaughtering of animals for food:*
"Then shall you slaughter of your herd and of your flock," Deut. 12:21.

Although not described in the Bible, ritual slaughter is one of the central elements of kashrut. Ethical considerations stressing the importance of compassion and respect for all living things led to creating humane methods of animal slaughter, methods that were designed for quick and painless death. Exactly what is involved in ritual slaughter and what else is done to meat to make it kosher will be discussed in detail in chapter 4.

KOSHER AND NONKOSHER ANIMALS

Permitted Mammals	Forbidden Mammals
Animals that both chew a cud (ruminants) and have a slit or cloven hoof, including: antelope, buffalo/bison, cattle, deer, eland, gazelle, goat, hart, moose, ox, sheep, yak	camel, dog, dolphin, donkey, horse, pig, porpoise, rabbit, rodents, whale

Permitted Fowl	Forbidden Fowl
Birds that have a projecting claw, a crop, and a gizzard or stomach whose inner lining can readily be peeled; most domestic fowl, including: capon, chicken, Cornish hen, duck, dove, goose, pigeon, songbirds, squab, turkey	Wild birds or birds of prey, including: eagle, heron, ostrich, owl, pelican, stork, swan, vulture

Permitted Fish	Forbidden Fish (Partial list)
Must have both fins and scales that are removable without damaging or tearing the fish's skin; 75 species including: anchovy, bass, blackfish, bluefish, butterfish, carp, chub, cod, flounder, fluke, haddock, halibut, herring, mackerel, mahimahi, mullet, perch, pickerel, pike, pompano, porgy, red snapper, sablefish, salmon, sardine, shad, smelt, snapper, sole, tilefish, trout, tuna, weakfish, whitefish, whiting	catfish, eel, lamprey, marlin, rays, puffer, sailfish, shark, sturgeon, swordfish, turbot All shellfish and mollusks, including: clam, lobster, octopus, oyster, scallop, shrimp, snail, squid

	Also Forbidden
	Reptiles, invertebrates, and amphibians, including: crocodile, frog, lizard, snake, toad, turtle, worms All insects

The dietary laws of kashrut divide all foods into two categories: kosher (Hebrew *kasher*), or permitted, foods and *trayf* (sometimes spelled *terayfa* or *treif,*) food that is unfit or improper to eat. (From the Hebrew word for "torn" or "damaged," *trayf* originally meant "torn from a wild beast" and therefore unfit to be eaten.)

Kosher or permitted foods are then divided into three categories:

1. **Dairy (milchig):** milk and all its derivatives, excluding milk from nonkosher animals. (Labels on dairy products are marked "-D-" after the symbol of kosher certification.)

2. **Meat, including poultry (fleishig):** from permitted animals (ones that chew their cud, generally cows and sheep) and have split hooves, that have been ritually slaughtered, and have undergone the koshering process of soaking and salting to remove any residual blood (see chapter 4). This procedure, which is also referred to as kashering, must be done under the supervision of a mashgiah, or rabbinic supervisor. (Labels on meat and poultry products are marked "-M-" after the symbol of kosher certification. An -M- may also mean that the product was processed on equipment that was used to process meat products.)

3. **Neutral (pareve):** foods that are neither dairy nor meat. Based on the verses in Genesis (1:29–30) in which God gives Adam and Eve permission to eat "every seed-bearing grass" and "every fruit-bearing tree," everything that grows in the ground is considered both intrinsically kosher and pareve. This includes, in their natural state, all plants, herbs, grains, fungi, fresh fruits and vegetables, flowers, roots, seeds, and nuts, as well as food products made from them, such as sugar, tea, flour, coffee, spices, pasta, salt, oils, and most condiments.

However, once a fruit or vegetable has undergone any form of processing, it may no longer be either pareve or kosher, since a nonkosher ingredient, or meat or dairy ingredient, may have been added. For example, coffee beans and ground coffee are pareve, but flavored coffees may not be, since they may include nonkosher or dairy ingredients. Similarly, canned tuna fish processed in water or oil would be pareve, but some tuna fish is processed with milk byproducts and therefore would be considered dairy. Also pareve are eggs (from kosher birds), as long as there is no blood in the yolk, and fish with fins and scales. Unlike kosher meat and poultry, kosher fish need not be killed by a ritual slaughterer, nor is it soaked and salted. (Labels on pareve foods have neither a -D- nor an -M- after the symbol of their kosher certification.)

For Orthodox Jews, pareve foods may be eaten with both meat and dairy foods. Because of the biblical injunction against "seething [cooking] a kid in its mother's milk," observant Jews do not cook or eat meat and milk together at the same time. Depending on local traditions, they also wait between three and six hours (about the time it takes to digest meat) after a meat meal before eating any milk or milk products. (If the dairy is eaten first, there is no need for this waiting period.)

Because they may be made of porous materials that allow particles of meat or dairy to be absorbed, cooking utensils and dishes have also come under this dietary law. Observant Jews have at least two sets of pots, pans, plates, bowls, knives, forks, etc.—one for milk dishes and one for meat. For the same reason they have two sets of dish towels and two separate bars of soap for washing dishes. In this way, they can be sure that there is no inadvertent mixing, however small, of meat and milk. Pareve foods can be cooked and eaten on either meat or dairy plates and utensils.

Although observant Jews consider fish to be pareve, it is not mixed with meat or poultry. This is another example of how sometimes enigmatic biblical injunctions were elaborated by later rabbis. The admonition to "verily guard your souls" was interpreted by Talmudic scholars to mean that you should closely guard your health, and therefore fish and meat should not be consumed together because you might not be scrupulous in looking for fish bones when eating the latter and therefore might choke on one.

Foods that are prohibited by the laws of kashrut are called *trayf,* and will never be found in food products that have been certified as kosher. They include:

- Meat from pigs, dogs, rabbits, horses, camels (four-footed animals that do not chew their cud).

- All insects.

- Rodents, reptiles, and creeping animals such as worms, snakes, and lizards.

- Invertebrates and amphibians, such as frogs and toads.

- Shellfish and mollusks.

- Animal blood.

- Certain sinews and fat, even if from kosher animals.

- Products such as gelatin and bone meal that are derived from prohibited animals.

- Any limb that has been cut or torn from a living animal (a graphic example of the biblical admonition against "causing pain to any living creature").

- Meat from any animal that has been killed by another animal or that died a natural death (one more extension of the prohibition against eating the flesh of an injured animal; also, such animals could not have been ritually slaughtered).

- Any food or food product that mixes milk, or milk products or derivatives, with meat or products derived from meat (of special importance for lactose-intolerant individuals and vegetarians).

WHAT MAKES A PRODUCT KOSHER?

1. Even though kosher foods already meet safety standards set by the U.S. Department of Agriculture (USDA) and the Food and Drug Administration (FDA), they also must meet certain additional requirements of Jewish law pertaining to raw materials and processing. Although there are three main branches of Judaism—Orthodox, Conservative, and Reform—it is Orthodox rulings that usually determine what is kosher.

2. Rabbinic inspectors and other members of kosher certifying agencies are trained specialists; they include food and flavoring chemists and processing experts, as well as authorities on kosher law.

3. All the ingredients in a processed food or product must be certified as kosher. This includes all of the raw materials as well as flavorings, colorings, stabilizers, etc. that are added to a processed food. (Certain additives, such as those derived from civet cats (civet), beavers (castoreum), and whales (ambergris), are intrinsically nonkosher. Others such as glycerin, gelatin, enzymes, emulsifiers, and fatty acids may be derived from kosher or nonkosher sources.)

4. Before a kosher endorsement is given to a product, the plant in which it is manufactured—the equipment it is processed on, as well as the container or packaging it comes in—must be inspected by a representative of the endorsing agency. Traces of nonkosher substances can remain on machinery and processing equipment and can be absorbed into the food, affecting its aroma and taste. If the equipment was previously used for nonkosher items, it must be washed with caustic soap and sterilized with boiling water before kosher products can be processed on it.

5. Even after a product is deemed kosher and receives certification, regular unannounced on-site inspections are made. Kosher inspectors have access to a company's records and storerooms, as well as plant machinery. In some instances, such as in meat and poultry slaughterhouses and processing plants, there may be a kosher supervisor or supervisors on duty at all times, around the clock.

6. Kosher meat and poultry must be ritually slaughtered and butchered, and prepared for the consumer by the prescribed method of salting and soaking.

CHAPTER TWO

UNDERSTANDING THE KOSHER SYMBOLS

Once you have decided to look for kosher products, you need to become familiar with the different symbols, called hechshers, that are used to designate kosher. More than two hundred and seventy organizations and individuals in the United States issue kosher certifications, and each has its own kosher symbols. A number of these certifying agencies, however, are regional groups or local rabbis.

Generally, when shopping for processed and packaged foods, the average consumer will need to recognize the symbols of the four major national certifying organizations. These four groups tend to share the same high standards for certification and are likely to accept each others' certification for ingredients and suppliers. They all employ experts in food chemistry, flavor processing, factory engineering, and food transport technology, as well as experts in religious law. Their supervision system extends worldwide, since they provide certification for companies that produce key raw materials and ingredients. The following symbols, used by the major certifying organizations, are registered trademarks:

A circle with a U in its center, often called the "OU," is the symbol of the Union of Orthodox Jewish Congregations, 333 Seventh Ave., New York, NY 10018, 212-563-4000. This is the largest kosher certifying agency in the world, a not-for-profit public service program for kosher certification that supervises more than two thousand companies in the United States and sixty countries overseas, and certifies over eighty thousand brand names, hotels, restaurants, companies, products, and services.

The Union, which was founded in 1898, supervises approximately 70 percent of U.S. kosher products. They publish a yearly *Consumer Directory of Kosher Products* ($10.00) listing companies, products, and services under their supervision, and a yearly *Kosher Industrial Directory* which lists all the industrial and food service products that they certify.

A circle with a K in its center, known as the "OK," indicates certification by the Organized Kashrus Laboratories, 1372 Carroll St., Brooklyn, NY 11213, 718-756-7500. Founded in the 1930s, the OK has 150 rabbis who certify over 600 companies on six continents. Their state-of-the-art computer system keeps track of all the ingredients in all the products they certify. The OK publishes a bimonthly magazine, *The Jewish Homemaker* ($2.95), which includes their "Kosher Food Guide of Products."

A letter K within the Hebrew letter *kof*, the first letter of the word *kasher*, indicates certification by Kosher Supervision Services, 1440 Queen Anne Rd., Teaneck, NJ 07666, 201-837-0500.

The so-called Kof-K is an international organization of Orthodox rabbis and experts in kosher food production. They were the first kashrut organization to introduce computer technology to kosher supervision and management. The Kof-K issues a *Guide* to their certified kosher products.

A five-pointed star with a K in its center (Star-K) indicates certification by the National Council of Young Israel and the Orthodox Jewish Council Vaad Haskashrus of Baltimore, 7504 Seven Mile Lane, Baltimore, MD 21209, 410-484-4110. This not-for-profit service issues a quarterly, *Kashrus Kurrents,* and a *Kosher Food Guide.*

In addition to the symbol of the certifying agency, the labels of kosher products also indicate their dairy, meat, or pareve status. Products marked "D" either contain diary ingredients or have been processed on equipment that is also used to process dairy products. Products marked "M" either contain meat ingredients or have been processed on meat equipment. If neither a D nor an M appears by the product name, that product is considered pareve.

The Generic K

Some products on supermarket shelves are marked with a simple K symbol, but this tells you little or nothing about their true kosher status. A letter of the alphabet cannot be trademarked or copyrighted in the United States. Although the Food and Drug Administration permits use of the K for kosher whether or not there has been rabbinic or kashrut supervision of the product, the simple letter K only means that the *manufacturer* claims the product is kosher. The generic K is not as reliable as other symbols since it offers no clue as to who actually certified the product or according to what standards. If consumers have a question about a generic K, they should inquire from the manufacturer for more specific information about the actual rabbinic supervision. More than fifty individual rabbis and local rabbinic authorities also use the K as their certifying symbol. (Their names and credentials are usually available from the product's manufacturer.)

Twenty-two states, however, do have consumer protection laws regarding kosher labeling.[1] In New York State, for example, the law requires that any kashrut symbol, including the K, must have a rabbi or supervising agency backing it, and *that* individual or organization must be registered with the state's Department of Agriculture.

---

1. Arizona, Arkansas, California, Connecticut, Georgia, Illinois, Kentucky, Louisiana, Maryland, Massachusetts, Michigan, Minnesota, Missouri, New Jersey, New York, Ohio, Pennsylvania, Rhode Island, Texas, Virginia, Washington, and Wisconsin.

In New Jersey, a law passed in November 1994 provided that a K or kosher claim must be backed up by posting the name of the certifying organization in each establishment, or the food producers must file a thorough disclosure form and prominently post a sign describing just what kosher standards were adhered to. Failure to keep the standards can be deemed a fraud and be fined by the state. For further information on these state laws, contact:

In New York State: Kosher Law Enforcement Advisory Board of the N.Y. State Department of Agriculture and Markets, 55 Hanson Pl., Brooklyn, NY 11217, 718-722-2852, fax 718-722-2836.

In New Jersey: The Kosher Enforcement Division of the Office of Consumer Affairs, 124 Halsey St., Newark, NJ 07101, 201-504-6375, fax 201-648-3139.

Local and Individual Symbols and Organizations

There are more than two hundred and seventy certifying agencies and individuals in the United States. Here is just a sampling of their symbols. These and other city, state, and regional organizations are often the ones that certify local restaurants, markets, butchers, and catering facilities. Some of these groups issue their own publications and lists of kosher products.

Atlanta Kashruth Commission, 1855 Vista Rd., Atlanta, GA 30329, 404-634-4063.

Kosher Overseers Association of America, P.O. Box 10209, Beverly Hills, CA 90213, 213-870-0011.

Rabbinical Council of Bergan County, 175 Van Nostrand Ave., Englewood, NJ 07631, 201-871-4620.

ORB   Orthodox Rabbinical Board of Broward & Palm Beach Counties, 7040 W. Palm Meadow Park Rd., Boca Raton, FL 33433, 407-391-1971.

Sephardic Rabbinical Council of America, 2030 Ocean Pkwy., Brooklyn, NY 11223, 718-376-0009.

Houston Kashruth Association, 9001 Greenwillow, Houston, TX 77096, 713-723-3850.

Chicago Rabbinical Council, 3525 W. Peterson Ave., Chicago, IL 60659, 312-588-2141.

Vaad Hakashrus of Cleveland, c/o Jewish Community Federation of Cleveland, 1750 Euclid Ave., Cleveland, OH 44115, 216-566-9200.

Vaad Hakashrus of Denver, 1350 Vrain St., Denver, CO 80204, 303-629-5159.

Certified Kosher Underwriters, 1310 48th St., Brooklyn, NY 11219, 718-436-7373.

Rabbinical Council of California, 617 S. Olive, Los Angeles, CA 90014, 213-489-8080.

Kosher Supervision of America, P.O. Box 35721, Los Angeles, CA 90035, 310-282-9444.

Mid-Atlantic Orthodox Rabbis, 1401 Arcola Ave., Silver Spring, MD 20902, 301-649-2799.

Vaad Harabonim of Massachusetts, 177 Tremont St., Boston, MA 02111, 617-426-6268.

Twin Cities Rabbinical Kashruth Council, 4330 W. 28th St., Minneapolis, MN 55416, 612-920-2183.

Rabbi Joseph H. Ralbag, 225 W. 86th St., New York, NY 10024, 212-595-7966.

Orthodox Vaad of Philadelphia, 7505 Brookhaven Rd., Philadelphia, PA 19151, 215-473-0951.

 Vaad Harabonim of Queens, 90-45 Myrtle Ave., Glendale, NY 11385, 718-847-9206.

Orthodox Rabbinical Council of San Francisco, 1851 Noriega St., San Francisco, CA 94122, 415-564-5665.

Kashruth Inspection Services of the Vaad Hoeir of St. Louis, 4 Millstone Campus, St. Louis, MO 63146, 314-569-2770.

Texas K Kosher Supervision, 3010 LBJ Freeway, Ste. 905, Dallas, TX 75234, 214-247-1042.

Rabbinical Council of Greater Washington, 7826 Eastern Ave. NW, Washington, DC 20012, 212-291-6052.

Kosher Supervisors of Wisconsin, 2700 N. 54th St., Milwaukee, WI 53210, 414-422-5730.

CHAPTER THREE ❧

THE GROWTH OF KOSHER CERTIFICATION

The market for kosher food has grown dramatically in the last ten years, expanding, it is estimated, at a rate of 15 percent annually. Today's consumers are much more health conscious than those of a generation ago. The public is increasingly aware of potential food contaminants: news stories about such events as the deadly outbreaks of "mad cow disease" in Great Britain and the *E. coli* infections in Japan and the United States make headlines around the world. For many people, a kosher certification is perceived as an extra level of quality assurance and good manufacturing procedures for the products they buy. For them, "kosher" has become equated with wholesomeness and purity.

Virtually every major food and beverage company has therefore turned to kosher certification—at least for some of their products—as a means of improving their market share in this highly competitive industry. Kosher food and products—nationally known brands and supermarket private labels—can now be found on store shelves all across America. A number of supermarket chains have specific kosher food sections in their stores.

For large manufacturers, the cost of kosher supervision—an average of about $3,000 to $6,000 per plant per year—does not show up in the retail prices they charge for dairy or pareve items. They often absorb the certification cost into their advertising and marketing budgets. This saving to the consumer does not occur with kosher meat and poultry, which can be much more expensive than their nonkosher counterparts, due to the labor-intensive methods of slaughter and preparation (to be discussed more fully in chapter 4).

How Certification Is Obtained

When companies seek kosher certification, they agree to have their manufacturing plants and products open to sometimes constant supervision. Kosher investigators or supervisors, called Mashgiah,[1] may have their own set of keys and can make unannounced on-site inspections, visiting plants more frequently than federal investigators do.[2]

The mashgiah is particularly concerned about the ingredients that go into a product and the machinery on which it is manufactured. Machinery which has been used to produce nonkosher products, or that once processed meat products and is now to process dairy products (or vice versa), must undergo a special kosher cleansing that may go beyond the cleaning procedures companies generally use.

Every single ingredient that is used in the food or comes in contact with the food—no matter where it is produced—must undergo the same thorough investigation.[3] This means that there

---

1. The mashgiah need not be a rabbi (although all Orthodox and Conservative rabbis must master a detailed knowledge of the laws of kashrut before they can be ordained). Any observant Jew trained to look out for kashrut problems can give certification. Kosher inspectors and supervisors must be well versed in the laws of kashrut as set down in a detailed 576-page text written in Hebrew and Aramaic, as well as in contemporary knowledge about food chemistry and processing.

2. The Food and Drug Administration, which inspects food processing plants (other than meat or poultry, which is the province of the U.S. Department of Agriculture), may visit once a year or less.

3. Food labeling laws allow for a certain ambiguity regarding ingredients. A "natural flavor" may actually contain more than one hundred different flavor components, including flavor-enhancing animal derivatives from such nonkosher animals as beavers (the extract castoreum) and civet cats. Carmine food coloring is derived from the pulverized shells of a beetlelike insect. Flavorings may also contain biotechnologically produced ingredients processed with such nutrients as blood or animal tissue.

Other examples of hidden ingredients are soya flour, which may be treated with an enzyme derived from the stomachs of swine; varieties of vegetable shortening containing emulsifiers—which allow two substances to be mixed together—that may be derived from animals; emulsifiers in baked goods, chocolates, and candies that may be glycerides derived from nonkosher animals rather than of vegetable origin; meat tenderizers containing lactose, a dairy ingredient; and creamers labeled "nondairy" that state and federal regulations allow to contain a small percentage of milk fat.

are kosher inspectors in almost every country in the world. This attention to ingredients extends to processing aids such as pan liners and release agents (used in baking) and to the containers and wrappings, which must also be certified, because minute amounts of chemicals in them can leach into the food.

Since many companies that manufacture kosher products also produce nonkosher ones, the same machinery may be used for different products or lines. If the supervisor finds that a piece of equipment was used for a nonkosher product, it must undergo a specific and stringent cleaning process overseen by the mashgiah. This includes a thorough washing with a caustic soap and sterilizing the equipment with boiling water. Equipment may also be disinfected with heat from blowtorches or steam guns.

Although kosher inspectors are not primarily looking for cleanliness, if they find that food has come in contact with a nonkosher ingredient such as bugs, rodent hairs, or droppings, they will deny it certification.

SOME MAJOR FOOD MANUFACTURERS THAT HAVE OBTAINED KOSHER CERTIFICATION FOR THEIR PRODUCTS

Note: The kosher status of companies and products can change; always check labels for current kosher certification.

Amway Corporation	Hershey's Chocolate Co.
Arrowhead Mills, Inc.	Horowitz-Margareten
Beatrice Foods	Hunt-Wesson, Inc.
Ben & Jerry's Ice Cream	Keebler Co.
Best Foods	Kellogg's
B. Manischewitz & Co.	Kraft-General Foods Co.
Borden	La Choy Food Products Co.
Carvel Corporation	Nabisco Biscuit Co.
Celestial Seasonings Inc.	Pillsbury
Chock Full O'Nuts Corporation	Procter & Gamble
Coca-Cola Bottling Co. of New York	Quaker Oats Co.
Dannon Co.	Rokeach Foods
Del Monte Corporation	Stella D'Oro Biscuit Co.
Dowbrands, L.P.	Stuckey's
General Foods Corporation	Thomas J. Lipton
General Mills	Tropicana Products, Inc.
Great Atlantic & Pacific Tea Co.	U S Mills
H J Heinz	

National Brands With Kosher Certification

Note: This is by no means an all-inclusive list of kosher products. Consumers should also be aware that the kosher status of products can and does change, so they should carefully check labels for current certification. The same caution applies to the dairy or pareve status of products. If readers have any question about the kosher designation of a specific item, they should contact the manufacturer or the certifying agency, or consult with their rabbi.

Baby Care Products

Adwe Laboratories/Dr Fisher's Nursery Line (shampoos, soapless soap, creams, sunscreen)

Baby Foods

Alsoy, Beech-Nut, Gerber, Heinz, Similac

Baking Mixes and Baking Products

Arm & Hammer baking soda, Arrowhead Mills bread mixes, Betty Crocker, Bisquick, Duncan Hines, Goodman, Keebler Francaise dough for puff pastry, Old Fashioned Kitchen Crepe Shells, Pepperidge Farm pastry shells and pastry sheets, pillsbury

Beverages and Drink Mixes

A&W Cola, Canada Dry, C&C Cola, Ceres Fruit Juices, Coca-Cola, Coors beers, Dr. Brown's beverages, Droste cocoa, Dr Pepper, Fruitopia, Holland House mixes, Hawaiian Punch, RC Cola, Seagram's club soda, ginger ale, seltzer, tonic water, Shasta sodas, Snapple natural teas, soda, seltzers, Tab, Tropicana citrus juices

Breads, Muffins, and Rolls

Arnold, Devonsheer, Entenmann's, Kemach breadsticks, Kineret frozen challah, Lender's bagels, Levy's, Mrs. Butterworth, Pepperidge Farm, San Luis sourdough breads and bagels, Sara Lee, Stella D'oro, Stroehmann's, Thomas's, Weight Watchers

Cakes and Pies

Drakes, Entenmann's, Heisler's, Pepperidge Farm, Pillsbury

Cereals and Grains

Arrowhead Mills organic flours, Back to Nature Flakes and Granola, Casbah flavored rices, Eden Foods whole wheat and quinoa flours, Energy Food Factory Uncle Roy's Cereals, Familia, General Mills cereals: Cheerios, Cocoa Puffs, Total, Wheaties, Kellogg's cereals: Corn Flakes, Froot Loops, Nutri-Grain, Rice Crispies, Kemach cereals and flours, Maypo, Nabisco cereals: Shredded Wheat, Cream of Wheat, Near East rice mixes, Quaker cereals: Cap'n Crunch, Instant Oatmeal, Puffed Wheat, Post cereals, Sahara Natural Foods couscous mixes, Sovex Natural Foods Good Shepherd cereals, U.S. Mills Cereals: Skinner's Bran, Erewhon brand cereals, Wheatena

Cheese Substitutes

Formagg cheeses, Soyco Parmesan cheese, Soymage cheeses, ToTuFu soy cheeses

Chinese Food Products

Canton chow mein noodles and egg roll skins, China Pack's duck sauces and hot mustards, Kemach chow mein noodles, La Choy Chinese vegetables: bamboo shoots, water chestnuts, sprouts, chow mein, other noodles, Mrs. Adler's hoison and soy sauces, Seasons Oriental vegetables, Wonton Foods wonton skin dough, egg roll skin dough, fortune cookies

Chocolates and Candies

Baby Ruth, Barricini chocolates, Barton's, Cadbury bars, Chuckle's, Ghiradelli chocolates, Glenny's 100% natural candies, Godiva chocolates, Hershey's Kisses, M&M's, Nestlé bars, Peter Paul Almond Joy and Mounds, Reese's Peanut Butter cups and pieces, Schrafft's, Sorbee hard candies, Starbucks, Stuckey's log rolls, Toblerone milk chocolates

Cleansers, Detergents, and Soaps

Ajax, Amway products, Arm & Hammer bleaches and detergents, Cascade, Cheer, Cinch, Clorox, Dow Oven Cleaner, Electrasol automatic dishwashing detergent, Fab, Fantastik, 409 cleaners, Hagarty silver cleaners, Ivory Snow, Kleen Bright, Lysol, Mr. Clean, Palmolive, Rokeach kitchen soap, Spic and Span, Sunbright

Coffee

Chock Full O'Nuts, Folgers, General Foods international coffees, Gillies certified organic coffees and natural decaf coffees, International coffees, Maxwell House, Medaglia d'Oro, Sanka instant coffee, Starbucks coffees, Taster's Choice instant coffees, Yuban

Condiments

B&G Relishes, Blanchard & Blanchard mustards, French's mustards, Gold's horseradish, Grey Poupon mustard, Heinz relishes, Ortega salsas, Westbrae mustards

Cookies and Crackers

Devonsheer melbas, Drakes, Duncan Hines, Entenmann's, Girl Scout cookies, Keebler cookies, Parco cookies, Pepperidge Farm cookies, Stauffer's, Stella D'oro, Steve's Mom rugelach, Walker's shortbread, Westbrae natural cookies

Cosmetics and Beauty Products

Cinema Beaute lipsticks, Maxx bath oil beads, Reflections cosmetics, Shain Dee lipsticks, blush, foundation, eye shadow

Creamers

Carnation Coffee-mate, Hershey's Non Dairy Creamer, Rich's Creamer

Dairy Products

Boursin spiced gourmet cheeses, Breakstone's butter, cream cheese and sour cream, Breyers Yogurts, Carnation milks,

Dannon yogurts, Farmland Dairies, Friendship Dairies, Kinor cheeses, Maggio ricotta cheeses, Miller's cheeses, Parmalat, Philadelphia Brand cream cheeses, Polly-O ricotta cheeses, Sealtest cottage cheese, sour cream, Sorrento mozzarella and ricotta cheeses, Taam Tou cheeses: American, cheddar, Gouda, mozzarella, Muenster, Swiss, Tuscan Dairies

Egg Products and Substitutes

Better 'n Eggs, Egg Beaters, Egg Watchers, Ener-G Egg Replacer, Wonderslim fat and egg substitute

Fish Products

Brunswick herring, kipper snacks and sardines, Bumble Bee tuna fish and salmon, Chicken of the Sea tuna, Empress anchovies, Season salmon, sardines, anchovies, tuna, Starkist tuna, Vita herring

Greek Food Products

Athens frozen spinach and cheese filos, Baklava, Spanakopita, filo, and strudel leaves, Krinos feta cheese and Greek olives, Oasis frozen moussaka, stuffed grape leaves, and nondairy spinach pie

Ice Cream, Sorbets, Ices, Frozen Yogurt

Ben & Jerry's, Borden ice cream, frozen yogurt, sherbert, Breyers ice cream and ice milk, Dannon frozen yogurt, Dolly Madison ice cream, Edy's ice cream and frozen yogurt, Friuli Sorbet, Frozfruit, Good Humor, Häagen-Dazs ice cream and frozen yogurt, House of Flavors ice cream, frozen yogurt, Howard Johnson, I Can't Believe It's Yogurt, Klondike, Mama Tish's Italian ices, Rosati Italian ices, Schrafft's ice cream, Sealtest ice cream, Sedutto ice creams and sherberts

Jams, Jellies, and Preserves

Hero preserves, Knott's Berry Farms, Kraft Foods jellies and preserves, Polaner, Roadside Farms, Tiptree preserves

Japanese Food Products

Eden Foods brown rice, miso, sea vegetables, soba and other traditional noodles, rice crackers, teas, wheat-free tamari and shoyu sauces, pickled Japanese vegetables, Erewhon miso, ramen, soba, nori, tamari, rice vinegar, teas, candies, seaweeds, Great Eastern Sun wheat-free tamari, umeboshi plums and paste, seaweeds, Mitoku Company sea vegetables, umeboshi products, dried shitake mushrooms, brown rice mochi, soba, udon and ramen noodles, sesame oils, rice crackers, wheat free tamari and shoyu sauces, teas, Mrs. Adler's tamari and teryaki sauces, San-J International teriyaki sauce, organic wheat-free and reduced-sodium tamari, Sobaya organic soba, udon, and sumen noodles, Westbrae Natural Foods miso, rice wafers, rice cakes, wheat-free tamari, instant miso soup

Margarine

Blue Bonnet, Fleischmann's, Imperial, Parkay, Promise, Superbrand, Weight Watchers

Mayonnaise

Best Foods, Chadalee Farms, Hellmann's, Kraft, Weight Watchers

Meat Substitutes

Green Giant Harvest Burgers, Lightlife Foods meat substitutes, White Wave meatless meat products, Worthington Foods meat substitutes

Mexican Food Products

Azteca corn and flour tortillas, La Mexicana tortillas and burritos, Ortega tostada and taco shells

Oils and Shortenings

Bertolli olive oil, Colavita olive oil, Crisco, Kraft oils, Liberty oils, Mazola oils, Pastorelli oils, Ribolzi olive oil, Wesson oils

Pancake and Waffle Mixes

Aunt Jemima, Hungry Jack, Manischewitz potato pancake mix, Pillsbury

Pan Coatings and Cooking Sprays

Butterbuds, Mazola NoStick, Pam No Stick cooking sprays

Pasta and Noodles

Bartenura gnocchi, Cemac Foods organic wheat-free dry pasta, Contadina, Creamette, DeBoles pastas, Don Peppe pastas, Eden Foods organic pasta, Goodman's noodles, Italpasta, Kemach noodles, Manischewitz noodles, Mueller's, Prince, San Giorgio, Sapore Di Napoli pasta, Vitelli pasta

Peanut Butter

Jif, Peter Pan, Planters, Reese's, Skippy

Pharmaceuticals, Over-the-Counter Drugs

Adwe Laboratories non-aspirin pain reliever, antacid tablets, heartburn relief tablets, and Adwe-Tussin, Celestial Seasonings throat lozenges, Luden's throat drops

Pickles and Pickled Products

B&G, BaTampte, Claussen, Heinz, Vlasic

Poultry and Poultry Products

David Elliott organic chicken, Empire Kosher Poultry, Galil kosher poultry, Hebrew National, Royal kosher poultry, Wise 'n Natural organic poultry

Private Labels

Many supermarkets chains have their own private or store labels for processed foods and food wrappings. Among the chains that have received kosher certification for a number of their private label products are Finast, Food Emporium, Foodtown, Grand Union, King Kullen, Pathmark, Shoprite, and Waldbaum's.

Salad Dressings

Blanchard & Blanchard, Cains, Chadalee Farms dressings, Heinz dressings, Henri's, Hidden Valley Ranch, Kraft Miracle Whip dressings, Nasoya Vegi dressings, Newman's Own, Pfeiffer, Weight Watchers

Sauces

Contadina marinara sauce, Heinz sauces, Hunt-Wesson barbeque sauces, Kemach pasta sauces, Kraft barbecue sauces, Lea & Perrins steak sauces, Manischewitz tomato and marinara sauces, Ortega Taco sauces, Red Wing sauces

Snack Foods

Charles' Chips, Flavor Tree, Frito-Lay corn chips and Ruffles, Gabilla & Sons knishes, Garden of Eatin organic corn chips, Keebler Pretzels, Konricko rice & wheat cakes, Mrs. Maltz knishes, Newman's Own popcorns, Nutri-Grain bars, Orville Redenbacher's popcorns, Pringles, Quaker rice cakes, Synder's of Hanover chips & pretzels, Uncle Roy's granola bars, Westbrae Natural Foods rice cakes, Wise chips

Soups and Soup Mixes

Goodman, Manischewitz, Rokeach, Tabatchnick's

Spices and Seasonings

Bac*os bits, Bacon Bits—imitation, Corona spices, Durkee spices and blends, La Flor spices, McCormick spices, Mrs Dash, Tones spices

Sweeteners

Draper's honey, Dutch Gold honey, Equal, Karo syrup, NutraSweet, Sweet 'n Low

Teas

Bigelow Teas, Celestial Seasonings teas, Lipton, Nestea, Remeteas herbal teas, Tetley, Uncle Lee's teas

Tomato Products

Furmano's tomato products, Heinz tomato ketchup, paste, puree, sauce, crushed tomatoes, Hunt-Wesson tomato products, Pomodora tomato products, Redpack tomato products, Red Wing tomato products, San Benito catsup, puree, crushed, stewed tomatoes, Westbrae ketchup

Toothpastes and Mouthwashes

Amway Anti-Plaque Fluoride toothpaste, Kosher Dent toothpaste, Lander mouthwash, Melaleuca tooth polish, mouth and throat sprays and washes, Shakelee New Concept dentifrice, Tom's of Maine additive-free toothpastes

Toppings

Betty Crocker, Hershey's, Pillsbury, Reddi Wip, Rich's non-dairy topping

Vegetable and Fruit Products

Bodek kosher produce, Del Monte dried fruits, Eden Foods organic beans and tomatoes, Green Giant canned vegetables, Heinz vegetarian baked beans, Hero canned fruit, LeSueur canned vegetables, Libby canned vegetables, National Produce fresh packaged vegetables, Seneca canned fruits and vegetables, Spratés vegetable spreads, Sun Giant raisins and nuts

Vitamins, Nutritional Supplements, Diet Aids

Boost, Ensure, Freeda Vitamins (no wheat, yeast, gelatin, salt starch, sulfites, preservatives), General Nutrition Products/Diet Center vitamins and mineral tablets, Kyolic garlic tablets and liquid, Landau children's and adults' vitamins (no sugar, starch, salt, milk, dyes, or additives), MaxiHealth Research vitamins, mineral and herbal supplements, vegetarian capsules, Naturemax energy boosters, Shakelee vitamins and nutritional supplements, Slimfast and Ultra Slimfast, Sunrider International vitamins and nutritional supplements, Sustacal, Twin Labs vitamins, minerals, food supplements, sports supplements

Wrappings and Paper Goods

Alcan foil products, Chinet molded dishes and trays, Glad wraps and storage bags, Hefty freezer and storage bags, James River Dixie cups and plates, Reynolds Cutrite wax paper, aluminum foil pans and foil, plastic film, Sweetheart Cup Company paper plates and cups, White Star paper cups and plates

CHAPTER FOUR

MEATS AND POULTRY

Because of the costly and time-consuming steps involved in their breeding, slaughter, and processing, kosher meats and poultry are notoriously more expensive than their nonkosher counterparts. But many people are willing to pay higher prices for the extra assurances that a kosher certification brings to these products.

To be considered kosher, meat and poultry has to satisfy a number of conditions (called shehitah) that go beyond what is mandated by the U.S. Department of Agriculture for meat on sale in the United States. These conditions include:

&· The meat must come from an animal considered kosher; that is, the animal for slaughter must be a permitted one. Animals for slaughter must be in apparent good health. Diseased animals are automatically considered nonkosher.

&· Kosher poultry must be raised without hormones or growth stimulants.

&· Animals cannot be artifically stunned before slaughter.[1] Nor can they be slaughtered mechanically, but must be dispatched by a shohet, a specially trained, ritual slaughterer, by the most painless and humane way possible. Because of the strength needed, shohets are generally male.

---

1. USDA regulations permit livestock and poultry to be stunned before slaughter with blows to the head, electric shock, or tranquilizer injections. None of these methods are permitted by kosher ritual.

Although the shohet need not be a rabbi, he is considered a religious official, knowledgeable about Jewish law, skilled in the theory and practice of slaughter, and one whose piety has been attested to by a rabbi. The knife used by the shohet is razor sharp and extremely smooth, it must not have any visible notches so that it will cut cleanly and quickly. The knife, which is twice as long as the width of an animal's throat, is checked for nicks or dents before and after each animal is slaughtered. If the blade shows any imperfection or if a hair or a feather clings to it, the animal can be declared ritually unfit for consumption and therefore will not get a kosher certification. If the imperfections are found before slaughter takes place, the knife must be resharpened before the shohet can continue.

ஃ Before the slaughter, the shohet recites a blessing. Then, because the animal must be killed instantaneously, he slits the animal's throat, severing the jugular vein, trachea, and esophagus in a single uninterrupted stroke. No stabbing motions or any pressure can be used. Even a momentary delay or the least bit of hesitation will make the killing invalid. This method of slaughter cuts off the blood supply to the animal's brain almost at once. Pain is thought to be minimized, and the animal loses a huge amount of blood immediately.

ஃ In order to ensure the wholesomeness of the meat, immediately after slaughter the animal's lungs and other internal organs are checked by a trained inspector, called a *bodek*, for any physiological abnormalities, discolorations, or symptoms of disease. Meat with certain types of adhesions, cuts, or bruises is rejected. There are over seventy defects that render an animal unsuitable. These include perforated or punctured organs, underdeveloped organs, organs of abnormal size, absence of an organ, internal cuts and bruises, hernias, fractured bones, dislocated limbs, infections, and tumors.[2] If the animal or bird is found to suffer from an illness or defects that would lead to its natural death within a year, its carcass is rejected.

Some kosher meat and other kosher products carry the designation "glatt kosher." Glatt refers to the perfect smoothness of an animal's lungs. The term has also come to mean "extremely kosher."

〰 Certain blood vessels, nerves, and lobes of fat in beef, veal, and lamb are forbidden by Jewish dietary law and are removed from the carcass.

〰 After slaughter, all the remaining blood must be extracted to fulfill the biblical injunction against consuming blood. The carcass is first hung, neck down, so that the blood drains freely. Then it is butchered into the permitted cuts and all the internal organs and parts are removed.

Next comes the koshering or kashering process, which is generally done for consumers by a kosher butcher before cutting and packaging the meat, although it can be done at home by the consumer. For poultry, the kashering process is completed at the slaughterhouse or packaging plant.

First, the meat or poultry is washed and soaked, totally covered, in clean cool water for half an hour. (The internal organs have already been removed and are koshered separately.) It is then placed on a perforated surface or on a flat grooved board set on an incline to drain, before being salted on all sides with coarse kosher

---

2. Many animals approved by the USDA for human consumption are unacceptable for kosher use. For example, USDA regulations allow nontumerous parts of a chicken to be sold: a chicken leg may be approved even if that chicken had a tumor on another part of its body. In order to be kosher, a chicken can have no tumors.

Also, USDA standards do not address questions about in what conditions the chickens were raised or what they were fed.

salt.[3] For poultry, both the inside and outside of the bird are salted. Coarse-grained salt is a very effective method for drawing off blood; regular table salt is too fine and would dissolve before it could have any effect on the meat. Finally, after an hour, the meat is rinsed off twice, again in cool water.

Liver, because it is so rich in blood, cannot be koshered in this manner. It must be broiled over a grate or an open flame. Hearts must be sliced open before being salted, to facilitate draining. For observant Jews, the rule about not consuming blood extends to eggs as well. If an egg has even a minute spot of blood in the yolk, it is discarded.

ﺰﻮ All meat and poultry must be koshered within three days of slaughter, because after seventy-two hours blood becomes so coagulated that it cannot be properly removed. Freezing meat after slaughter also prevents the blood from draining. Ground meat cannot be koshered, so meat used for hamburgers and the like is koshered before grinding.

ﺰﻮ Supervision of the koshered meat and poultry continues until the product reaches the consumer. Meat and poultry must be properly tagged and labeled. For fowl, a metal tag, called a *plumba*, bearing the kosher certification, serves as an identifying seal. Kosher butcher shops and markets also must be under kosher supervision.

Note: A free 22-page brochure, "Make It Kosher Meat," is available from the New York Beef Industry Council, P.O. Box 250, Westmoreland, NY 13490. Send a stamped, self-addressed envelope. The brochure contains basic information on cooking kosher cuts, recipes, and strategies for maintaining a healthy diet that includes meat.

---

3. A note to those on sodium-restricted diets: According to the New York Beef Industry Council, experiments performed by the New York State Department of Agriculture and Markets indicated that the penetration of salt from the koshering process is less than ⅛ inch from the surface.

Kosher Salt

Although chemically identical to other salts that come from the sea or from dried salt beds (sodium chloride), kosher salt differs from regular table salt in several ways. It is large-grained, light, and flaky, contains less salt per teaspoon, and adheres better to food. (While there are table and sea salts that are certified as kosher, the term "kosher salt" refers specifically to the large-grained variety.)

Table salt is made by driving water into a salt deposit and evaporating the brine that is formed, leaving dried cubelike crystals that resemble granulated sugar. Kosher salt is made in the same way, but during the evaporation it is continuously raked, giving it a lighter, flakier texture. Kosher salt also differs from its counterparts in that it has no additives such as iodine, often added to table salt to prevent goiter and as an anticaking agent.

Kosher salt can be used as a general kitchen salt. Many professional chefs prefer it for cooking and seasoning, believing that the additives in regular table salt can give food an "off" taste.

Two nationally available brands of kosher salt are Morton's Coarse Kosher Salt and Diamond Crystal Kosher Salt.

A Guide to Kosher Meats

Jewish dietary laws mandate the removal of certain arteries, veins, nerves, and sinews from animals before they can be eaten. These include the sciatic nerve and its accompanying blood vessels which run through the hip joint and hindquarters of cattle and sheep. Genesis 32:33 prohibits eating this nerve in remembrance that Jacob was touched on the thigh's sciatic nerve when he wrestled with the angel. From this biblical story, Talmudic scholars and rabbinic interpreters drew various conclusions, including proof that God would not allow the annihilation of the Jewish people.

Removal of the sciatic nerve is an extremely time-consuming and therefore expensive process, so in the United States, the hindquarters of kosher animals are usually sold to nonkosher butchers. However, some kosher butchers will undertake the tedious job of removing the sciatic nerve and some specialty shops do sell kosher filet mignon, kosher leg of lamb, and so forth.

The kosher and nonkosher cuts of beef, veal, lamb, and poultry are:

BEEF	
Kosher Cuts **(from forequarters)**	**Nonkosher Cuts** **(from hindquarters)**
Brisket	Loin
Chuck (ground, filet steak, pot roast)	Rump
Breast flanken, rib flanken,	Shank
Minute steak, cubed steak	Flank
Rib top	Filet mignon
Delmonico cut	Sirloin
Short rib	Tenderloin
Standing rib roast	T-bone
Shoulder roast, shoulder steak,	Porterhouse
hanger steak	
Rib eye, rib steak	
Skirt steak	
Round (ground, steak, pot roast)	
Tongue	

VEAL	
Kosher Cuts **(from forequarters)**	**Nonkosher Cuts** **(from hindquarters)**
Breast	Loin
Cutlets	Flank
Shoulder, shoulder steak	Leg
Rib (chops, roast)	Hind Shank
Brisket	
Tongue	

LAMB	
Kosher Cuts (from forequarters)	**Nonkosher Cuts (from hindquarters)**
Neck	Loin
Shoulder chops	Leg
Shank	
Rib (chops, roast)	
Breast (roast, brisket)	

POULTRY
Kosher
All parts of chicken, Cornish hen, duck, goose, pigeon, turkey, capon

A Note on Islamic Dietary Laws

Islam, the Muslim religion, also divides foods into those that are permitted, referred to as *halal*, and those that are *haram*, or forbidden. As in Judaism, forbidden foods include blood and pig and pork products. Also forbidden are animals that have not been slaughtered in the proper manner, (that is, by cutting the jugular vein with a very sharp knife while reciting a prayer pronouncing the name of Allah (God). Surah 2:172 in the Koran, the Muslim holy book, forbids eating "an animal that dies of itself, and blood and the flesh of pigs, and that on which any other name has been evoked beside that of God."

Like the Torah, the Koran forbids the eating of birds of prey, rodents, reptiles, and insects, except locusts. However, unlike Jews, Muslims are permitted to eat camel meat. Meat from kosher butchers is considered *halal*, or proper for consumption.

These dietary restrictions are an important obligation for Muslims. In a 1987 study of Islamic values in the United States, 90 percent of American Muslims responding said they never ate pork or pork products, and two-thirds believed that it was important to buy and eat *halal* meat whenever possible.

Chicken the Kosher Way

Chicken is America's number-one meat. Since 1975, the annual per capita consumption of poultry has doubled to more than seventy pounds per adult. According to the National Broiler Council, Americans eat 500 million pounds of chicken and turkey each week, and approximately 4 million pounds of that is kosher poultry.

In a number of blind taste tests sponsored by food and cooking magazines, kosher chickens invariably beat the leading supermarket poultry brands and came out at or near the top when compared to other speciality premium brands. Many experts say kosher chickens do have a different taste, a result, perhaps of the extra steps kosher poultry processors take in the breeding, feeding, raising, and processing of their chickens, turkeys, and ducklings.

For example, the chickens bred by Empire Kosher Poultry of Mifflintown, Pennsylvania, the world's largest producer of kosher chickens, are free-roaming, rather than caged for their entire lifetimes. In bad weather they are housed in brightly lit, environmentally controlled sheds. Galil Poultry of Livingston Manor, New York, raises its chickens on a special scientifically devised high-protein, all-natural diet of grain, soybeans, corn, wheat germ, and naturally occurring minerals. Empire also has its own rabbinically supervised feed mills and hatcheries. Indeed, all aspects of kosher poultry's growth and processing—from egg-laying conditions to transportation and slaughter, to the dressing, wrapping, and shipping of the product to market—are overseen by rabbinic supervisors.

Feed for kosher fowl contains no growth stimulants, antibiotics, hormones, or preservatives. In contrast, many of the chickens destined for processing by the industry giants are fed a "least-cost formulated diet," which changes as the market price for the various ingredients fluctuate. This feed may also contain additives, preservatives, byproducts, or fillers forbidden by kosher laws.

Most chickens in the United States are slaughtered at six or seven weeks. Kosher chickens are allowed to "grow out," that is, they are permitted to grow to full maturity, slowly and naturally, and are not shipped to the processing plant until they are at least nine weeks old.

Once kosher chickens arrive at the processing plant, each one is checked for signs of illness and to see if it sustained any injuries during transport. If so, it is immediately rejected. All kosher poultry is hand-held to be slaughtered; the birds cannot be stunned electronically beforehand, nor can they be slaughtered by machine. The salting process is also done by hand; other aspects of processing are done on high-tech conveyers and soaking vats. The finely honed knives used by the shohets, the ritual slaughterers, are constantly being checked to see that they are razor sharp, because any irregularity or minor imperfection in the blade is thought to cause the animal additional suffering, something forbidden by Jewish law. Because their job requires such intense concentration, the shohets work only for an hour at a time.

In addition to the standard inspections done by USDA workers (who only began inspecting poultry processors in 1958), mashgiah, or kosher supervisors, are stationed all along the production line, continually checking for external and internal defects and diseases that would make a bird unfit for the kosher market. Kosher inspectors are much stricter than those who work for the USDA, and reject more poultry as inedible than the government does. Birds are rejected for such things as punctured organs, abnormal growths, and certain broken bones that would pass USDA inspection.

U.S. Department of Health regulations call for the removal of all feathers from processed poultry to prevent the spread of bacterial-borne disease. Nonkosher processors make this difficult job easier by soaking their birds in hot water. Kosher chickens cannot be processed in hot water because technically that would begin to "cook" the bird before it was properly koshered. So kosher processors use cold, fresh running water for all washing and rinsing—a process, incidentally, that has been shown to help retard the growth of bacteria and to prevent cross contamination.

It takes approximately three hours from slaughter to packaging of a kosher chicken. The U.S. industry average for all poultry is forty-five minutes.

Note: Empire Kosher Chicken maintains a Customer Hotline to answer cooking questions and to provide information on product availability. They also offer free company literature and recipes. Empire can be contacted at 800-367-4734, Monday through Thursday, 8 A.M. to 5 P.M. Eastern Time, or Friday, 8 A.M. to 3 P.M.; or at Web site http://www.empirekosher.com or by E-mail at empire@acsworld.net.

CHAPTER FIVE

WINE AND SPIRITS

> Wine is sure proof that God loves us and wants us to be happy.
>
> —BENJAMIN FRANKLIN

Mention kosher wine and for many people the adjectives that come to mind include "sweet" and "heavy." But kosher wine is no longer limited to the traditional "sacramental" red wines made from New York's Concord grapes.[1] In the past ten years it has taken on a whole new look and taste. More than a dozen wineries in California, New York, France, Italy, and Israel have begun producing kosher varietals, including some award-winning, top-ranked Chardonnays, Cabernet Sauvignons, and white Zinfandels.

Wine, often thought of as a symbol of joy, redemption, and hospitality, plays an important role in Jewish celebrations and holidays such as Passover. Special prayers are said over wine before Sabbath meals. Genesis 9:20–21 tells us that the first thing Noah did after the Flood was to plant a vineyard. The Psalms (104:15) speak of "wine that maketh glad the heart of man."

How Wine Becomes Kosher

Although other kosher foods and beverages may be prepared or manufactured by non-Jews as long as there is proper supervi-

---

1. Jewish immigrants arriving in the United States who needed to make kosher wine for their religious ceremonies found that the only grapes available were a local variety known as Concord. With a high-acid, low-sugar content, these grapes were unlike the ones they had known in Europe. To compensate for the differences and to balance the natural acidity, the winemakers added sugar during processing. The result was the sweet syrupy drink that many people still associate, erroneously, with all kosher wines.

sion and certification, special rules apply to kosher wines. Since biblical times, wine has been an important part of religious rites and ceremonies, and therefore special prodedures need to be taken in order for it to be considered kosher. For example, from the time the grapes are crushed to the moment the product is bottled and corked, the wine and the winemaking equipment may be handled only by Jews who observe the Sabbath (sundown Friday to sundown Saturday).[2]

Other rules must also be followed:

- Although the grapes used for making kosher wine are no different from those used to make nonkosher wines, they cannot be picked on the Sabbath or on Jewish holidays such as Rosh Hashanah, Yom Kippur, or Sukkot (which, unfortunately, usually fall right in the middle of the prime grape harvesting season).

- Juices are fermented using kosher yeast and enzymes that do not contain *any* animal-derived ingredients. No animal-derived products can be used in any part of the winemaking process. This includes the soaps used to clean the tanks and barrels as well as the fining (purifying) and filtering agents. Since there are no commercial kosher bacteria, vinters have to make their own cultures from natural yeasts found in the air and on the grapes themselves—an expensive and time-consuming project.

- Cleanliness is of the utmost importance: the fermenting tanks, barrels, hoppers, pumps, and presses are sterilized with purifying chemicals or steam jets and rinsed

---

2. Some kosher wines have the word "Mevushal" on their label; in Hebrew the word literally means cooked or boiled wine. Mevushal wines, which have been flash-pasteurized at high temperatures before bottling, can be uncorked and poured by anyone—observant Jew or Gentile—and still be considered kosher. For Orthodox Jews, this "cooked wine" is no longer officially considered wine and therefore, like other kosher foods and products, can be handled by anyone and still keep its kosher status. (This ruling goes back to biblical times, when boiled wine was considered unfit as a sacramental offering.) Flash-pasteurization does not affect the taste or quality of the wine.

with 190-degree water before the grapes are crushed. The barrels have to be cleaned three times.

❧ The entire process has to be overseen by a mashgiah or religious supervisor.

Other alcoholic beverages that contain grape wine, such as certain liquors, arak, brandy, champagne, cognac, sherry, vermouth, and sangria, must comply with the above rules in order to be certified kosher.[3] Alcoholic beverages and spirits such as beer, unflavored grain vodkas, rye, bourbon, and Scotch (straight and blended), which are grain or potato based, are considered inherently kosher and pareve, as are true fruit liquors, unless they contain flavorings and additives or grape products or derivatives. If so, their production must be under kosher supervision.

A Selection of Kosher Wines and Spirits

A number of companies and wineries produce or import kosher wines and spirits. The following is a sampling of what is available in the United States.

Canandaigua Wine Company, New York

Abarbanel brand
    Beaujolais, Cabernet Sauvignon, Chardonnay
Manischewitz brand
    Blackberry wine, Chardonnay, Cream Almonetta, Cream peach, Elderberry, Loganberry, Malaga, Medium Dry Concord

Carmel Wine Company, Israel

Founded in 1882, today Carmel is a cooperative of two hundred winegrowers.

Carmel sparkling wines
    Blanc de blancs, Brut reserve cuvée, Sparkling Chardonnay

---

3. Grape products (or products that contain wine, grape derivatives, or grape flavoring), such as jams, jellies, grape juices, candies, and wine vinegar, also must receive kosher supervision.

Carmel Valley wines
  Cabernet Sauvignon, Colombard, Grenache Rosé, Sauvignon Blanc, Sémillon
Carmel Vineyards wines
  Cabernet Sauvignon, Chenin, Dry Muscat, Emerald Riesling, Sauvignon Blanc, Shiraz, White Zinfandel
Rothschild wines
  Cabernet Sauvignon, Chardonnay, Ermerald Riesling, Merlot, Sauvignon Blanc, White Muscat
        Carmel also produces a number of brandies and dessert wines, vodkas, and cream liqueurs.

Gan Eden, Napa, California

Sauvignon Blanc, Chenin Blanc, Black Muscat, Chardonnay Reserve, Cabernet Sauvignon, Sémillon, Gewürztraminer

Hagafen Cellars, Napa, California

Cabernet Sauvignon, Chardonnay, Chardonnay Reserve, Harmonia red and white table wine, Johannesburg Riesling, Pinot Noir, Pinot Noir Blanc

Royal Wine Corporation, Brooklyn, New York

Baron Herzog wines, California
  Blush Muscat, Cabernet, Cabernet Sauvignon, Champagne Brut, Chardonnay, Chenin Blanc, Red Zinfandel, Sauvignon Blanc, Special Reserve Chardonnay, White Zinfandel
Bartenura wines, Italy
  Amaretto, Asti Spumante, Chianti Classico, Lambrusco, Merlot, Pinot Grigio, Sambuca, Soave, Valpolicella
Gamla, Golan Heights, Israel
  Cabernet Sauvignon, Chardonnay, Muscat, Sauvignon Blanc, Special Reserve Cabernet
Herzog French wines
  Baron Rothschild Haut Médoc, Beaujolais Villages, Cabernet Sauvignon, Chardonnay, Château de la Grave Bordeaux, Château Grande Noyer Pomerol, Château la Rèze Minervois, Châteauneuf semi dry white, Chinon, Muscadet

J. Furst, California
  Cabernet Sauvignon, Chardonnay, Fumé Blanc, Pinot Noir,
  White Zinfandel
Kedem, New York State
  Burgandy, Chablis, Concord, Malaga, Sauternes, Sherry,
  Tokay
Weinstock, Sonoma, California
  Cabernet Sauvignon, Chardonnay, Gamay, Sauvignon Blanc,
  White Zinfandel

Note: The Royal Wine Company publishes a kosher wine
newsletter, *From the Grapevine.* A free copy is available by writing to the company at 418-A Kent Ave., Brooklyn, NY 11211.

Yarden, Golan Heights, Israel
Cabernet Sauvignon, Sauvignon Blanc, Chardonnay, Mt.
Hermon red and white, Merlot, White Riesling, Port Blanc,
Champagne Brut

Other kosher wines are produced by Mount Maroma,
Rutherford, California (Chardonnay, Cabernet Sauvignon);
Fortant de France (Merlot, Chardonnay); Pays d'Oc, France
(Cabernet Sauvignon, Merlot, Chardonnay, Sauvignon Blanc);
George Duboef, France (Beaujolais); Rashi, Italy (Moscato
D'Asti, Prumasco Cortese white, Prumasco Barbera red); Naveh
Vineyards, Elgin, Arizona (Sonoita Sauvignon Blanc); Kojafa,
Denmark (cherry and peach wines).

The following spirits, hard liquors, and beers have also
received kosher certification: Stolichnaya vodka, Finlandia
vodka, Cristall, Priviet, Godiva liquor, Ginjo Premium Sake, Sho
Chiku Bai sakes, Takara Mirin beer, Coors beers and lagers,
Cherry Heering liqueur, Disarono Amaretto liqueur, Sabra
liqueurs, Leroux liqueurs and schnapps, Old Williamsburg
Bourbon, Montaigne cognacs, and Hamashkeh Scotch.

Note: The California Winemakers Guild, 800-858-9463
(24 hours) can provide bimonthly shipments of wine produced
by small kosher wineries from around the world. Each shipment
includes an informative newsletter.

CHAPTER SIX

KOSHER AND HEALTHY

Are kosher foods healthier than nonkosher foods? Many people think so, but the answer to that apparently simple, straightforward question is yes/no/sometimes. Junk food can be kosher; "natural" foods purchased in health food stores may contain nonkosher ingredients. And while a kosher diet eliminates fatty pork products including lard, and bacon, it doesn't necessarily exclude fatty processed meats such as salami or bologna, or baked goods made with coconut or palm oil, both high in saturated fats.

Although the original intent of the dietary laws set forth in the Bible and Talmud were religious and ethical, not medical, they may have given those who followed them unexpected health benefits in the centuries before refrigeration, knowledge of germs and bacteria, and government inspection and regulation of food. The noted Jewish philosopher and physician Maimonides (1135–1204 C.E.) claimed in his *Guide for the Perplexed* that kosher foods were indeed healthier to eat. (And, sounding more like a modern fitness guru than a medieval doctor, Maimonides advocated a diet that emphasized exercise, whole grains, and fresh fruit. He also advised moderation in the use of alcohol, and warned about eating too much fat, pastries, and salty meat and cheese.)

Examples of the unintended and unexpected health benefits from "keeping kosher," still applicable today, might have included the following:

ë Among the "unclean" animals prohibited by kosher laws are those that were frequently fed leftover, possibly moldy, food. Today we know that some molds produce aflatoxins, which, when ingested by humans, can cause infections and diseases. There have also been reports of high aflatoxin concentrations in bacon and lard, and in slaughtered pig carcasses.

The ban against eating pork might also have led to a lower incidence of trichinosis. Undercooked pork and pork products are a major source of this serious disease caused by eating foods infected by a parasitic roundworm.

ë The prohibition of shellfish, which sometimes grow and feed in polluted bottom waters, might also have had health benefits. Raw shellfish can contain naturally occurring toxins such as paralytic shellfish toxin; they can also cause illness from viruses, salmonella, or other bacterial infections. According to the National Academy of Sciences, "no other commercially available food poses a greater health risk." Raw shellfish, including oysters, mussels, and clams, account for 66 percent of the cases of food poisoning in the United States each year.

ë The koshering process—salting and washing—might have helped preserve meat in the days before refrigeration. (The ledger book of a cargo ship that sailed from Newport, Rhode Island, to the island of Jamaica in 1782 showed an entry for "Jew beef"—salted meat that had a kosher stamp on it.) Today we know that blood can carry disease. Kashering meat and poultry—draining it of blood—might also have lessened the incidence of blood-borne illness.

Other beneficial effects may also come from kashering. One study, reported in *Food & Cosmetic Toxology* (14:1, 1976), indicated that the salting and soaking process appeared to lessen the risk of the formation of nitrosamines, cancer-causing agents. Salting can also reduce or eliminate some types of bacteria, especially campylobacter, a common contaminant of poultry. It also appears to reduce the risk of salmonella (a leading cause of food-borne illness) in chicken. The U.S. Department of Agriculture estimates that as many as four thousand deaths and five million illnesses result annually from the consumption of meat and poultry contaminated with four major bacterial pathogens: salmonella, campylobacter, *E. coli* 0157:H7, and *Listeria monocytogenes*. While the koshering process helps kill or reduce these pathogens, the only way to completely guarantee the safety of kosher and nonkosher meat products is to follow a few simple rules of handling and cooking.

All meat sold in the United States is about to become safer to eat when it comes to bacterial contamination. As this book is being written, Congress has agreed to provide money to underwrite major changes in the nation's meat and poultry inspection system, modernizing ninety-year-old procedures based on looking, touching, and smelling. This is the so-called sniff-and-poke method, where Agriculture Department inspectors had only a few seconds to spot obvious signs of disease or spoilage as animal and bird carcasses sped by them on the assembly line.

But some health hazards are invisible to the human eye. The new system, which will be known as Hazard Analysis Critical Control Point, seeks to lessen the level of harmful bacteria, including salmonella. It will also include microbial testing (and quick computer analysis of the results) for *E. coli*, a potentially deadly fecal contamination. It is expected that 75 percent of the country's meat and poultry production will be under the new inspection laws by January 1998, with the remainder to follow by the year 2000. The new system and testings, however, will not completely eliminate the incidence of salmonella and campylobacter, but only reduce it.

Today, kosher products not only must meet safety standards set by the USDA and the Food and Drug Administration, they must also adhere to the sometimes even stricter laws of kashrut. Kosher supervisors visit food-processing factories more often than federal inspectors do. In the case of meat and poultry, kosher supervisors may reject twice as many animals as their nonkosher counterparts, adding an extra level of health and safety protection for the kosher consumer.

HANDLING MEATS AND POULTRY SAFELY

Even after the government's new systems for reducing the bacterial contamination of meat and poultry are in place, consumers should still follow the USDA's guidelines for safe food storage and preparation.

- After purchase, perishable foods such as fresh meat or poultry should be taken home immediately and placed in a refrigerator (at 40° F. or below) or freezer (0° F.). Food-borne bacteria multiply rapidly in the danger zone between 40 and 140 degrees.

- To avoid spreading bacteria ("cross contamination") from uncooked to cooked foods, after handling raw eggs, meat, fish, or poultry, wash hands and utensils with hot soapy water.

- Cook or microwave meat to a high internal temperature to kill harmful bacteria and/or parasites. Beef, including ground beef mixtures such as meat loaf or hamburgers, should be cooked to 160° F. or until brown in the middle and juices have no trace of pink. Steaks and roasts may be cooked to 145° F. (medium rare), 160° F. (medium), or 170° F. (well done). Lamb should be cooked to 170° F.; poultry, to 180–185° F. (juices should run clear); boneless turkey roast, to 170–175° F; veal, to 170° F; and fish to 140–145° F.

- For further information on food safety, consumers can call the USDA's Meat and Poultry Hotline at 800-535-4555.

Government Help for the Consumer

Whether you buy kosher or nonkosher foods, it is easier than ever to become a more savvy, health-conscious consumer. New nutritional guidelines and recent changes in government labeling regulations are helping make it so.

The Food Guide Pyramid

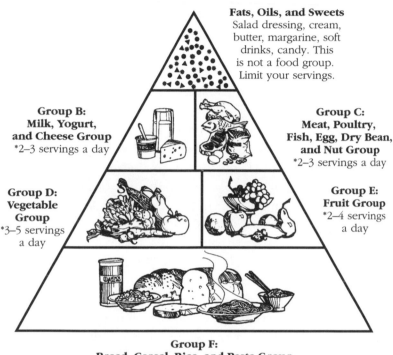

Fats, Oils, and Sweets
Salad dressing, cream, butter, margarine, soft drinks, candy. This is not a food group. Limit your servings.

Group B:
Milk, Yogurt, and Cheese Group
*2–3 servings a day

Group C:
Meat, Poultry, Fish, Egg, Dry Bean, and Nut Group
*2–3 servings a day

Group D:
Vegetable Group
*3–5 servings a day

Group E:
Fruit Group
*2–4 servings a day

Group F:
Bread, Cereal, Rice, and Pasta Group
*6–11 servings a day

Source: USDA; U.S. Department of Health & Human Services
*Sample serving sizes:

Group B: 1 cup low-fat milk or yogurt; 2 oz. processed cheese (preferably low-fat); 1½ oz. natural cheese (preferably low-fat).

Group C: 2–3 oz. cooked lean meat, poultry, fish; ½ cup cooked dry beans; 1 egg or 2 tbs. peanut butter equals 1 oz. lean meat. The leanest cut of kosher beef is round; most fish is considered lean; turkey or chicken with the skin removed is considered lean.

Group D: 1 cup raw leafy vegetable; ¾ cup vegetable juice; ½ cup other vegetables, cooked or raw.

Group E: ¾ cup fruit juice; ½ cup chopped, cooked, or canned fruit; 1 medium apple, banana, orange.

Group F: 1 muffin, 1 dinner roll or slice of bread; 1 oz. ready-to-eat cereal; ½ cup cooked cereal; rice; pasta.

Within the past few years, the USDA and the Department of Health and Human Services have revised their Food Guide Pyramid, a model of recommended daily food choices that emphasizes balance, variety, and moderation. With the variety of kosher products available today, eating healthy while eating kosher is not a problem.

There are also new federal labeling laws already in place that will help consumers make healthier choices in their food selections. These new laws were revised jointly by the Food Safety and Inspection Service of the USDA, the agency responsible for labeling meat and poultry, and the FDA, which is in charge of all other packaged goods.

Since the spring of 1994, when the 1990 Nutrition Labeling and Education Act became law, all packaged and processed foods in the United States (including all kosher foods) have been required to display a detailed list of ingredients and specific information on their nutrient content.[1] According to the National Food Processors Association, in 1996 more than a half million food packages carried the new labels.

There are a few exceptions to the new law. Some packages are allowed to have a short or abbreviated nutrition label. These include small or medium-size packages (less than 12 square inches available for labeling), which must then include an address or phone number of the manufacturer who may be contacted for information; plain coffee, tea, some spices, and other foods that are known to have no significant amount of any nutrient; foods that contain only a few of the nutrients that require listing; and infant formula. Also exempt are foods produced by some small companies; food served in restaurants, airplanes, hospitals, bakeries, delis, and retail establishments; and food sold by vendors in malls, on the street, or from vending machines.

Nutritional information may also be voluntarily displayed at the point of purchase for fresh fruits and vegetables. If

---

1. This includes processed meats such as hot dogs and breaded chicken cutlets. At the time of writing this book, however, the labeling of fresh poultry and meat is voluntary, and information may or may not be displayed at the point of purchase.

Nutrition Facts

Serving Size 1 cup (228g)
Servings Per Container 2

Amount Per Serving

Calories 260   Calories from Fat 120

	% Daily Value*
Total Fat 13g	**20**%
Saturated Fat 5g	**25**%
Cholesterol 30mg	**10**%
Sodium 660mg	**28**%
Total Carbohydrate 31g	**10**%
Dietary Fiber 0g	**0**%
Sugars 5g	
Protein 5g	

Vitamin A 4%	•	Vitamin C 2%	
Calcium 15%	•	Iron 4%	

* Percent Daily Values are based on a 2,000 calorie diet. Your daily values may be higher or lower depending on your calorie needs.

	Calories:	2,000	2,500
Total Fat	Less than	65g	80g
Sat Fat	Less than	20g	25g
Cholesterol	Less than	300mg	300mg
Sodium	Less than	2,400mg	2,400mg
Total Carbohydrate		300g	375g
Dietary Fiber		25g	30g

Calories per gram:
Fat 9 • Carbohydrate 4 • Protein 4

such information is posted and makes reference to the waxes and resins used to coat the produce, the laws mandate that the reference must indicate the *source* of the ingredients in the coating, rather than just its name. This is important for both kosher and vegetarian consumers, who would want to know whether the coating was derived from animals or plants.

Understanding the new nutritional labeling will help all consumers make knowledgeable choices about what they eat. The following is a brief look at the new labels and what important information can be gleaned from them.

The labels, headed "Nutrition Facts," must, by law, give the following information:

ë *Serving Size:* Although it is not necessarily a "recommended amount," serving size is based on a typical portion as determined through consumer surveys by the U.S. Government. The serving size is listed in both common household units, such as 1/2 cup, and in metric units—grams (g) and milligrams (mg). About 28 grams equals 1 ounce; 1,000 milligrams equals 1 gram. Serving sizes are the same for similar foods. For example, a serving of pretzels will be about the same size as a serving of potato chips. The amount of calories and the nutrients listed on the package are based on the serving size, so if you eat twice the serving size, you will get twice the calories and nutrients.

ë *Calories:* The number of calories in one serving and the number of calories derived from fat in one serving. Dietary guidelines recommend that people get no more than 30 percent of their calories from fat each day; some nutritionists think even that amount is too high.

ë *Percent Daily Values:* The amount, in one serving, of certain important nutrients including fat, cholesterol, carbohydrates, fiber, sugar, protein, sodium, and vitamins. Amounts for two key vitamins and two minerals must be included: vitamins A and C, calcium, and iron. If vitamins and minerals other than these four have been added or the product makes a claim about other vitamins or minerals, their percentage must also be listed. The nutrients are listed in two ways: (1) in terms of the amount by weight per serving (given in grams or milligrams), and (2) as a percentage of the daily value, a new nutrition reference tool. By using the Percent Daily Values, it is easy to determine whether a food contributes a lot or a little of a particular nutrient. A higher percentage means it contains a lot of that nutrient; a low percentage means it contains a little. If you eat twice the serving size indicated on the label, you are getting twice the *percentage* of daily value of nutrients.

The Percent Daily Value on all labels is based on a sample diet of 2,000 calories a day.[2] If your daily caloric intake is higher than 2,000, the food you eat adds a lower percentage of daily value to your diet. If you eat less than 2,000 calories, the food you eat adds a higher percentage. Another part of the label shows recommended total daily amounts (in grams and milligrams) for total fat, saturated fat, cholesterol, sodium, total carbohydrates, and dietary fiber, based on two sample diets, one with 2,000 calories, the other with 2,500.

A note on the nutrition portion of the label explains the 2,000-calorie basis for the percentages given. An individual's daily caloric needs depend on many factors, such as age, height, weight, and activity level. Whatever your caloric intake, the Percent Daily Value can be used as a reference to see how a particular food fits into the context of a total diet. For example, a diet of 1,500 calories a day is 75 percent of a 2,000-calorie diet; therefore

2. According to the FDA, a 2,000-calorie-a-day diet is generally recommended for most moderately active women, teenage girls, and sedentary men. Many older adults, children, and sedentary women need only 1,600 calories. A 2,500-calorie-a-day diet may be suitable or appropriate for many men, teenage boys, and active women.

the Percent Daily Values for each of the nutrients in all the foods you eat should total 75 percent instead of 100 percent. If one food provides 25 percent of the daily value for fat, all the other foods you eat that day should add up to no more than 50 percent.

&. *Ingredients:* If a product contains more than one ingredient,[3] it must carry a list that states all the ingredients in descending order of weight. The ingredients that make up less than 2 percent of the product can be noted in any order at the end of the ingredient list. This list is now required on almost all foods, even standardized ones such as mayonnaise, peanut butter, and bread, which previously did not need to carry an ingredient list. Natural flavorings and colorings can be listed just as "flavorings" or "colorings," and their source does not have to be given (although it may be). However, artificial flavorings and colorings must be identified as such. The source of an artificial flavoring does not have to be given, but a source must be listed for an artificial color: for example, Yellow #5.

Also, the total percentage of juice in juice drinks must be declared.

&. *The Front Label on the Package:* Many food labels and packaging carry health claims and claims about their nutritional content, such as "fat free" or "high in fiber." The new labeling laws have placed specific and legal limits on what manufacturers can claim about their products. The FDA is now allowing claims linking a nutrient or food to the risk of a disease or health-related condition in only seven cases where the link has been supported by scientific evidence. Products making a health claim must contain a defined amount of nutrients.

3. This refers to *added* ingredients. Exceptions are made for products such as mineral water: the mineral content does not have to be listed, since the minerals are considered an inherent part of the product, not added ingredients.

The only allowable health messages that a manufacturer may make are claims that show a link between (1) calcium and a lower risk of osteoporosis; (2) fat and a greater risk of cancer; (3) saturated fat and cholesterol and a greater risk of coronary heart disease; (4) fiber-containing grain products, fruits, and vegetables and a reduced risk of cancer; (5) fruits, vegetables, and grain products that contain fiber and a reduced risk of coronary heart disease; (6) sodium and a greater risk of high blood pressure, and (7) fruits and vegetables and a reduced risk of cancer.

In addition, terms that are used to describe a food's nutrient content are limited and now have strictly regulated definitions. Only certain terms are allowed: (**Note:** Standard serving sizes are assumed. For products with small serving sizes (30 grams or less or 2 tablespoons or less, the amounts permitted are smaller.)

- *Free*: The product must contain no amount or only a very small amount of the substance. For example: "calorie-free" means less than 5 calories per serving; "sugar-free" means less than 1/2 gram of sugar per serving; "fat-free" means less than 1/2 gram of fat per serving[4]; cholesterol-free" means less than 2 milligrams of cholesterol and 2 grams (or less) of saturated fat per serving; sodium- or salt-free means less than 5 milligrams of sodium.

- *Low:* Used in conjunction with fat, cholesterol, sodium, or calories. For example: low-fat means 3 grams[5] or less

---

4. Some "low-fat" or "fat-free" products make a claim that they are a certain percentage fat-free. This term will now have to accurately reflect the amount of fat present in 100 grams of food. Thus a food with 3 grams of fat per 100 grams would be "97 percent fat-free." Consumers should also note that fat-free products may contain more sugar and/or more sodium for improved taste. Therefore the caloric count may not be much lower than for comparable products that are not fat-free.

5. Late in 1996, the 1990 Nutrition Labeling and Education Act was amended to include milk and some dairy products (cottage cheese products and sour half-and-half, a lower-fat sour cream), that had been previously exempted by the FDA. Beginning in 1997, 2 percent milk, which has 5 grams of fat per serving, must now be called "reduced fat," not "low fat," as it has long been labeled. One percent milk, which contains 2.5 grams fat per serving, can qualify for "low fat," and skim milk, which has no fat at all, can be labeled "fat free" or nonfat." The new rules, however, do not apply to yogurt.

of fat per serving; low-sodium means 140 milligrams or less of sodium per serving; low-cholesterol means 20 milligrams or less cholesterol and 2 grams or less saturated fat per serving. Very low sodium means 35 milligrams or less sodium. Low-calorie means 40 calories or less per serving; and "low calorie meal" is 120 calories or less per 100 grams. Low saturated fat means 1 gram or less of saturated fat per serving and 15 percent or less calories from saturated fat.

ﻤ *Lean:* Used to describe the fat content of meat, poultry, or fish containing less than 10 grams of fat, less than 4 grams of saturated fat, and less than 95 milligrams of cholesterol per serving and per 100 grams.

ﻤ *Extra Lean:* Used to describe the fat content of meat, poultry, or fish containing less than 5 grams of fat, less than 2 grams of saturated fat, and less than 95 milligrams of cholesterol per serving.

ﻤ *High:* The product must contain 20 percent or more of the daily value for that nutrient per serving. High-fiber means 5 grams or more of fiber. If a food is not "low-fat," the label must declare the level of total fat per serving and refer to the nutritional panel when a fiber claim is mentioned.

ﻤ *Good Source of:* Indicates that one serving of the product contains 10 to 19 percent of the Daily Value for a nutrient. A "good source of fiber" contains 2.5 to 4.75 grams per serving. If a food is not "low-fat," the label must declare the level of total fat per serving and refer to the nutritional panel when a fiber claim is mentioned.

ﻤ *Reduced or Less:* The product contains less than 25 percent of a nutrient or calories when compared to a similar product. If a claim is made for "reduced cholesterol," the product must also have 2 grams or less of saturated fat per serving than a comparison food. Consumers should be aware, however, that like fat-free products, those with less fat or reduced fat may contain more sugar and/or more sodium for taste, and therefore may not be much lower in calories than comparable products.

ॐ *Light or Lite:* The product contains at least one-third fewer calories or at least 50 percent less fat than the higher-calorie, higher-fat version; or no more than half the sodium of the higher-sodium version. If a food derives more than half its calories from fat, fat content must be reduced by 50 percent or more. The adjective "light" can also be used to describe a food's texture or color, provided the intent is clear, as in "light brown sugar."

ॐ *More:* One serving provides at least 10 percent more of the Recommended Daily Value of a nutrient than a comparison food does.

Other familiar food packaging terms now also have specific meanings:

ॐ *Enriched and fortified:* The food has been nutritionally altered so that one serving provides at least 10 percent more of the Daily Value of a nutrient than the comparison food does.

ॐ *Fresh:* Generally used for food in its raw state, it cannot be used on food that has been frozen or cooked, or that contains preservatives.

ॐ *Fresh Frozen:* Can only refer to food that has been quickly frozen while still fresh.

ॐ *Unsalted:* No salt has been added during processing. To use this term, the product it resembles must normally be processed with salt and the label must note that the food is not a sodium-free food if it does not meet the requirements for "sodium-free."

For further information on the new labeling laws consumers can write or call, toll-free: the Food and Drug Administration, 5600 Fishers Lane, HFE-88, Rockville, MD 20857, 800-535-4555 (10 A.M.–4 P.M. Eastern Time) or to Food Safety Education, USDA, Food Safety and Inspection Service, Rm. 1180S., 14th St. and Independence Ave. SW, Washington, DC 20250, 800-FDA-4010 (24 hours, recorded information; agents, 12–4 P.M. Eastern Time).

Health newsletters and healthy eating guides are also available from:

Consumer Reports on Health
P.O. Box 52148
Boulder, CO 80322
800-234-2188

Eating Smart Guides and
Nutrition Action Newsletter
Center for Science in the
Public Interest
1501 16th St. NW
Washington, DC 20036

Harvard Heart Letter
P.O. Box 420235
Palm Coast, FL 32142-0235
800-829-9171

*Harvard Medical School Health
Letter*
P.O. Box 10945
Des Moines, IA 50340
800-829-9171

*Harvard Women's Health
Watch*
P.O. Box 420235
Palm Coast, FL 32142-0235
800-829-5921

Health News
P.O. Box 52924
Boulder, CO 80322
800-848-9155

*Johns Hopkins Medical
Letter*
P.O. Box 420179
Palm Crest, FL 32142
904-446-4675

Mayo Clinic Health Letter
P.O. Box 53889
Boulder, CO 80322
800-333-9037

National Health, Lung and Blood Institute and *National Cholesterol Education Program*
c/o National Institutes of Health
Bethesda, MD 20892

Tufts University Diet and Nutrition Letter
800-247-5470

University of California/ Berkeley Wellness Letter
P.O. Box 10922
Des Moines, IA 50340
800-829-9080

University of Texas Lifetime Health Letter
7000 Tannen DCT 12012
Houston, TX 77030
800-829-9177

🍀

CHAPTER SEVEN

KOSHER FOR VEGETARIANS

Vegetarianism[1] may be as old as the Bible, an ideal of the Garden of Eden, where no meat was eaten. In Genesis 1:29–30, God tells Adam and Eve, "Behold, I have given you every seed-bearing grass upon the face of the earth and every fruit-bearing tree, these shall be for you to eat. And to every beast of the earth and every bird of the sky and every creeping thing, to everything that has the breath of life in it, I have given the green grass for food."

It was only after God saw the corruption of Noah's descendants that the killing of animals for consumption was permitted: "Every moving thing which lives shall be yours for food, just as I have given you the grasses, so do I give you all" (Gen. 9:3). Even then, several passages in the Torah assert that it would be better to eat no meat at all. The Talmud credits the longevity of the generations from Adam to Noah as being due to their vegetarian diet.

German rabbi Samuel Raphael Hirsch (1808–1888), a leading Orthodox thinker, concluded that perhaps vegetarianism was preferable to meat eating, since the human body and the human mind are connected by the food one consumes, and plants are "the most passive of substances." "Anything which gives the body too much independence or makes it too active in a carnal direction," he wrote in "Hoeb: A Philosophy of Jewish

---

1. There are over 10 million vegetarians in the United States. The word itself is derived from the Latin for "to enliven." Many people believe that vegetarians are thinner, healthier, and live longer than nonvegetarians. Some actuarial statistics seem to bear this out.

Law and Observances," brings it nearer to the animal sphere, thereby robbing it of its primary function, to be the intermediary between the soul of man and the world outside."

Some people think the vegetarian lifestyle is a modern fulfillment of the goals of kashrut and Judaism.[2] If you must kill animals for food, the Jewish religion instructs, you kill them humanely. Following this logic, not killing them is the most humane act of all. And since meat is a resource-intensive food, for ecologically minded vegetarians, not eating meat helps conserve, rather than deplete, our resources.

While kashrut may form a philosophical basis for some vegetarians, kosher labeling and dietary laws can help all vegetarians better sort out the processed and packaged goods on supermarket shelves.

THE MOST COMMON TYPES OF VEGETARIANISM ARE:

	Does Not Eat	Emphasizes
Pescovegetarian	Red meat, poultry	Fish, plant foods
Pollovegetarian	Red meat, fish	Poultry, all plant foods
Ovolactovegetarian	All meat, fish, poultry	Eggs, milk, milk products, all plant foods.
Ovovegetarian	All animal foods except eggs	Eggs, all plant foods
Lactovegetarian	All animal foods except milk and milk products	Milk, milk products, all plant foods
Vegan vegetarian	All animal foods	Plant foods only

2. A vegetarian diet is an ideal also stressed by of several Eastern religions, including Taosim and Hinduism. Many Buddhists are vegetarians because their code, the Eightfold Path, calls for them not to harm living things. The two million Jains of India are strict vegetarians. They will not even eat root vegetables because the whole plant dies when the root is harvested for food.

Members of the Seventh-Day Adventist church, a now worldwide Protestant denomination formally established in America in 1863, are expected to adhere to the biblical principles of diet and health—in effect, the Jewish dietary laws. They abstain from alcohol and tobacco, and are encouraged to follow a vegetarian diet. It is estimated that half of the 7.7 million Seventh-Day Adventists are vegetarians.

How Kosher Labeling Helps

Because milk and dairy products cannot be combined or eaten together with meat, kosher products marked with a "D" (for dairy) contain *no* meat or meat products. Products labeled "pareve" (neutral) contain neither dairy nor meat. However, vegetarians who want to avoid eggs and fish still need to check the ingredient list, since these items are considered pareve.

For example, margarine sometimes contains animal fats or their derivatives. Margarine marked "pareve" would contain no such ingredients. Commonly used food dyes and flavoring agents may contain up to a hundred different chemicals and enzymes which do not have to be listed on the package. This includes flavors designated as "natural." Some of these chemically produced items are made from meat byproducts, including such items as civet, an enzyme derived from extract of civet cat, or beaver secretions (castoreum). The bright-red coloring agent carmine is extracted from insects.

A long list of food products—including margarine, shortenings, cream fillings and toppings, cake mixes, doughnuts, puddings, coffee creamers, ice cream, frozen deserts, instant mashed potatoes, peanut butter, and breakfast cereals—contain emulsifiers, substances that allow two ingredients to mix together, making oil and water soluble. On labels, emulsifiers—or, as they are sometimes called, stabilizers—may be listed as polysorbates, mono- and diglycerides, sorbitan monostearate, calcium stearol lactylate, magnesium stearate, or calcium stearate.

Although emulsifiers may be derived from either animal or plant/vegetable sources, the new federal laws do not mandate that the source of the emulsifiers be listed. Mention need only be made that emulsifiers have been added to the product. Pareve/vegetarian kosher products would contain emulsifiers such as lecithin, which come from a nonanimal source.

In addition, any kosher pareve or dairy product will not be wrapped in plastic or paper that contains any animal product or was made with any chemicals or oils using any animal byproducts. Some food plastic packaging uses beef tallow as a surface coating material. This tallow can interact with the contents of the package, so packaging certified as kosher would not contain this coating.

THE QUESTION OF GELATIN

Gelatin, a tasteless, odorless substance extracted from cattle or hog bones, hooves, and hides, is considered nonkosher by Orthodox dietary laws, even if the gelatin was derived from kosher animals (which is itself a very expensive process). Gelatin is an ingredient in many desserts, candies, frozen dairy products, baked goods, yogurt, sour cream, and cottage cheese. Kosher foods use vegetable gelatin substitutes, including agar-agar, a seaweed gel; carrageenan and Irish or Chinese moss, derived from algae; and vegetable gum, extracted from plants.

Kosher pharmaceuticals may also use a new type of fish gel in place of animal gelatin.

Vegetarian Groups and Magazines

Vegetarian Resource Group
P.O. Box 1463
Baltimore, MD 21203
410-366-VEGG
Web: http://www.envirolink.org/arrs/VRG/home.html
A nonprofit group that will answer questions about vegetarian diet. Publishes books as well as a monthly magazine, *Vegetarian Journal*.

American Vegan Society
P.O. Box H
Malaga, NJ 08328
609-694-2887

Natural Health Magazine
P.O. Box 57320
Boulder, CO 80322

North American Vegetarian Society
P.O. Box 72
Dolgeville, NY 13329

Vegetarian Times
P.O. Box 578
Oak Park, IL 60303
708-848-8100
800-298-0358

Veggi Life
1041 Shary Circle
Concord, Ca 94518
510-671-9852
Web: http://www.vegilife.com

CHAPTER EIGHT

FOR THE LACTOSE-INTOLERANT

Milk, in one form or another, is a hidden ingredient in thousands of different products, from processed foods such as TV dinners and canned tuna fish to candies and baked goods to vitamin pills and prescription drugs. But in the United States, more than 50 million people have a problem with milk. This includes infants and children who are allergic to milk protein and exhibit such symptoms as respiratory distress, abdominal pain, skin rashes, and eczema after eating or drinking milk or milk products.

An estimated 20 percent of American adults are lactose-intolerant, suffering either from a lactose deficiency or from lactose maldigestion. Lactose deficiency results from a partial or complete lack of an enzyme (produced in the small intestines) called lactase, which the body requires to digest lactose, the sugar found in animal milk. The symptoms of lactose deficiency, which occur after consuming milk or milk products, include often painful intestinal cramping, bloating, excess gas, and diarrhea.

As they age, most people gradually lose, in varying degrees, the ability to digest lactose.[1] Some adults can have no dairy products at all. Others can eat dairy foods in moderation. Depending on the severity of their condition, some individuals can drink milk if it is consumed with a meal or if it is fermented,

---

1. The ability to *tolerate* lactose in adulthood is probably a genetic mutation, since in most cultures (except Western European dairy societies), our ancestors did not drink milk after leaving early childhood.

as are cultured buttermilk and yogurt. Cheese, which is low in lactose compared to milk (.5 milligram per ounce versus 11 grams per ounce) can sometimes be eaten with no uncomfortable symptoms. Besides milk, the foods that cause the most problems are ice cream, cottage cheese, sour cream, ice milk, and frozen yogurt. Certain ethnic groups, including people of Asian, African, Native American, and Jewish descent, are more apt to have problems digesting milk as they grow older.

LACTOSE INTOLERANCE

It is estimated that 70 percent of the world's adult population suffers from lactose intolerance to some degree. Different ethnic groups, however, exhibit the condition in varying percentages, according to the Wisconsin Department of Health and Social Services:

	Percent
Africans	93
Japanese	92
Greek	87
Native Americans	83
Arabs	80
Eastern European Jews	78
African Americans	70
South Americans	65
Indians	56
Caucasian Americans	8

Consumers who want to avoid milk or milk products need to read labels carefully, since milk and its derivatives can be listed under a number of different names, including:

&. Whey (the liquid residue that remains when milk is curdled; contains both milk sugar and milk protein).

&. Casein (a milk protein, sometimes used in processing canned foods, including tuna fish).

&. Sodium caseinate (a milk protein).

&. Lactalbumin (a milk protein).

&. Lactoglobulin (a milk protein).

&. Calcium lactate (a crystalline salt, used in baking powder).

The Kosher Option

Buying kosher products is one option for those who are lactose-intolerant, lactose-maldigestive, or allergic to milk protein, allowing them to eat a variety of healthy foods safely.[2]

Since the kosher dietary laws prohibit the mixing of meat and milk, *all* kosher meat products are milk-free and do not contain even a trace of milk or milk products. For example, dried milk is a common ingredient in many nonkosher processed meats; some creamers labeled "nondairy" may in fact contain some dairy ingredients; additives such as monosodium glutamate (MSG) may contain a lactose filler. With pareve or neutral foods such as fish, fruits, and vegetables, if the kosher certification symbol is followed by a "D" it means that the product contains *some* milk or milk product and is therefore considered dairy. The same would be true of those "nondairy" creamers. However, there are kosher nondairy creamers that are completely dairy-free. These (such as Rich's Non Dairy Creamer) would have the certifying symbol followed only by the word "pareve." (A certification symbol followed by a "P," however, indicates that the product is kosher for Passover, the Jewish holiday during which no leavening is eaten. This "kosher for Passover" designation is of help to people who are allergic to wheat or wheat starch or who suffer from celiac disease and cannot tolerate the gluten found in wheat, oats, barley, and rye, since no grains can be eaten during Passover.)

Individuals who are lactose-intolerant or have lactose malabsorbtion can often eat yogurt (of which there are many kosher brands available) and acidophilus milk, which contains bacterium that increases the bacterial count in the stomach and intestines and eases the digestion of lactose. Several companies—including Anderson Erikson Dairy, Dairy Maid Dairy,

---

2. Dairy products are high in calcium, riboflavin, protein, phosphorus, and magnesium, which help protect against osteoporosis, a debilitating bone disease. Those who cannot eat dairy foods comfortably should increase their intake of nondairy calcium-containing foods such as dates, prunes, legumes, broccoli, leafy green vegetables such as kale and Chinese cabbage, canned salmon and sardines with the bones included, calcium-fortified soy milk, and tofu.

Dominick's Dairy, Louis Trauth Dairy, Muller Pinehurst Dairy, and Pensupreme—manufacture kosher acidophilus milk. Dynamic Health Laboratories of Brooklyn, New York, produces kosher (and pareve) liquid acidophilus in a variety of flavors. (Acidophilus milk tastes the same as regular milk, but it cannot be heated. Heat destroys the lactobacillus acidophilus bacterium.)

Kosher lactose-reduced milks (whole, skim, reduced-fat, and low-fat) are also available from a number of dairies. Among these products are Dairy Ease Lactose-reduced milks, Dairyman's Cooperative Creamery lactose-reduced skim milk, McNeil Consumer Products' Lactaid milks, and Ultra Dairy's Bodywide lactose-reduced nonfat milk. Lactaid also markets a lactose-reduced, low-fat cottage cheese.

There is also a kosher over-the-counter product available that helps the body break down lactose, making it easier to digest by supplying the lactase enzyme which the body lacks. Lactaid, which is available in caplet or liquid form, can be added to refrigerated skim or whole milk (it breaks down about 70 percent of the milk sugars after twenty-four hours in the refrigerator). Or it can be chewed along with the lactose-containing food. For further information and a sample caplet, call McNeil Consumer Products at 800-LACTAID (522-8243), 9 A.M.–5 P.M., Eastern Time.

Additional sources for information on lactose intolerance include the American Dietetic Association, 800-877-1600, and the National Osteoporosis Foundation, 800-223-9994.

The Dannon Company publishes a free booklet, "You Asked About Lactobacillus Acidophilus," which includes information on yogurt cultures and lactose intolerance. Send a stamped, self-addressed, legal-sized envelope to Dannon Information Center, P.O. Box 1102, Maple Plain, MN 55592.

For the National Dairy Council's brochure "Getting Along With Milk," send 25 cents along with a stamped, self-addressed envelope to National Dairy Council, Nutrition Services Department, 10255 W. Higgins Rd., Ste. 900, Rosemont, IL 60463.

For more information about calcium, call the Calcium Information Center, 800-321-2681.

Dairy Substitutes: Soy Milk and Tofu

Soy milk and tofu, popular with vegetarians, are versatile lactose-free substitutes that are available with kosher certification.

Soy milk is a rich liquid extracted from soybeans. Nutritionally complete, it supplies many of the same important nutrients as milk. All soy milk is high in protein (more so than cow's milk) and is also high in iron and vitamin B-12. Some soy milks are fortified with calcium, which is especially important for lactose-intolerant people who are also strict vegetarians and therefore never consume any animal products. Soy milk is available in low-fat and nonfat versions.

Tofu, also known as bean curd or soy cheese, is a relatively inexpensive yet complete and easily digestible food. A versatile form of high-quality protein, it is rich in calcium, vitamins, and minerals and is cholesterol-free. Tofu is made by heating soy milk to the boiling point, adding a curdling agent, and then separating the curds from the whey. The curds are then pressed together to make cakes of tofu.

Fresh tofu comes packed in water, and will keep for four to five days in the refrigerator; the water should be changed every day or two. Tofu can be frozen for up to three months in a well-sealed container. Frozen tofu develops a chewy, meatlike texture. Tofu is also available freeze-dried. To rehydrate this product (which can last indefinitely), pour boiling water over it.

An 8-ounce serving of tofu (about 144 calories) provides substantial daily calcium and protein requirements for an adult, as well as the B vitamin choline, which is needed by the brain. Tofu contains all eight essential amino acids. It is low in fat compared to cheese, and is free of cholesterol. A 1977 study cited in *The Lancet*, a British medical journal, reported that tofu even lowered cholesterol in people who had high levels, perhaps because it provides lecithin, which helps dissolve the artery-blocking substance.

Tofu comes in a variety of styles. Depending on its water content, it is designated Extra Firm, Firm, Regular, Soft, or Silken (the latter lends a creamy texture to sauces and desserts). Tofu, which is porous and bland, will absorb the flavors of what it is cooked or blended with. It can be prepared in a number of ways: broiled, deep-fried, sautéed, marinated, blended into sauces, or mashed into a spread. Kosher tofu can be served at any dairy meal.

Other soy-based products include soy flakes; soy flour; soy ice creams; soy powder; tamari (or shoyu), a rich dark, naturally fermented soy sauce that contains no added flavorings or caramel; miso, a concentrated high-protein paste made from soybeans and grains that, like yogurt, is rich in lactobacilli; and tempeh, a fermented food (made from cooked soybeans inoculated with a mold starter) that has a high protein and B-12 content.

A number of companies produce kosher soy and tofu based products. Among them are:

- Eden Foods, Clinton, Michigan: soy milk (carob, vanilla, or regular flavor), dried tofu.

- Global Protein Foods, Valley Cottage, New York: tofu.

- Leasa Tofu, Miami, Florida: fried and regular tofu.

- Lightlife Foods, Greenfield, Massachusetts: tofu, tempeh.

- Mitoku Co., Tokyo, Japan: snow-dried tofu.

- Mu Tofu, Chicago, Illinois: tofu, tempah, soy milk.

- Nasoya foods, Leominster, Massachusetts: tofu, tofu-based Veggi mayonnaise, tofu-based salad dresssings, San-J wheat-free tamari soy sauce, San-J low-sodium tamari soy sauce.

ᏽ Stow Mill, Chesterfield, New Hampshire: New England organic produce tofu.

ᏽ Tofutti Brands, Cranford, New Jersey: nondairy frozen desserts and mixes, nondairy cream cheese and sour cream.

ᏽ Westbrae Natural Foods, Commerce, California: miso.

ᏽ White Wave, Boulder, Colorado: reduced-fat tofu, baked diced tofu.

CHAPTER NINE

COOKING KOSHER

Cooking kosher can be adapted to many cuisines, tastes, and budgets. The thirty-three recipes I've included here—favorites from family and friends—represent dishes from Greece to Russia, from Israel to Portugal, from New York's Lower East Side to Louisiana's Cajun country.[1]

Most of these recipes are easy to prepare, although a few require some cooking expertise. I've included traditional Jewish foods (no collection of kosher recipes would be complete without one for chicken soup), adaptations from several international cuisines, and recipes that reflect today's health-conscious eating habits.

---

1. My special thanks to my mom, Beatrice Garfunkel, and to Florence Fialkoff, Lynn Kozbial, Maren Kozbial, Sandy and Gerry Muroff, Zena and Michael Muroff, Claire and Nat Muroff, Harry and Martha Pollack, and Joyce and Aaron Garvin.

Soups

Fruit Soup   Pareve

> 1 large cantaloupe
> 6 mint leaves (optional)
> 1 cup watermelon balls or cubes
> 1 cup honeydew balls or cubes
> 1 cup blueberries or sliced strawberries (optional)
> 1 cup diced peaches or diced mangoes (optional)

Cut the cantaloupe in half and remove the seeds. Scoop the flesh and any juice into a blender. Add mint leaves, if desired. Process until puréed. Set aside.

Combine the other fruits in a large serving bowl. Pour the purée over the fruit. Can be served at once or chilled.

Serves 6–12

Mom's Good-for-What-Ails-You Chicken Soup With Heavenly Light Matzo Balls   Meat

Practically every cuisine and culture has its own way of making chicken soup, but it is the version using kosher chickens that has come to be called "Jewish penicillin." Chicken soup's restorative and curative power has a long history. Centuries before modern scientific research suggested that hot chicken soup could indeed alleviate symptoms of colds and the flu, the twelfth-century Jewish physician and philosopher Maimonides recommended it both as a nourishing food and for its medicinal properties.

My mother's recipe makes, without prejudice, the best soup I've ever tasted (and also the best poached chicken). It's well worth the effort involved in its preparation. I've also included her recipe for never-fail, heavenly light matzo balls. Both soup and matzo balls freeze well.

For the Soup

> 1 4–5 pound kosher pullet (stewing chicken), quartered
> 4 quarts water
> 1 tablespoon kosher salt
> salt and ground black pepper to taste
> 1 large onion, peeled
> 3 large carrots, peeled and sliced
> 2 stalks celery, with tops
> 3 large parsnips, peeled and cut in half
> A handful of flat Italian parsley
> A bigger handful of fresh dill
> 4 chicken bouillon cubes

For the Matzo Balls

> 2 tablespoons corn oil
> 2 eggs, slightly beaten
> ½ cup matzo meal
> Pepper and salt to taste
> 2 tablespoons chicken soup stock or water
> 1½ quarts water
> 2 chicken bouillon cubes

Wash and skin the chicken quarters. Trim off excess fat.

Put the water in a large enameled or stainless steel pot, add the kosher salt, and bring to a boil. Add the chicken, cover, and simmer for about 1 hour. Every few minutes, skim off the foam that forms on top of the water—this will give you clear broth.

After the soup has simmered for about 1 hour, add the onion, carrots, celery, parsnips, parsley, and dill. Lower the flame and cook for approximately 45 minutes, covered. Then add the bouillon cubes and cook another 10 minutes. Remove the onion and discard. Remove the chicken and vegetables and set aside. Remove the dill and parsley and discard.

Let the soup cool a bit, then strain into another pot. Put the carrots back in the pot. Add salt and pepper to taste.

Before serving, place matzo balls (see recipe below) in the pot and heat.

To Make the Matzo Balls

Mix the oil and eggs. Add the matzo meal and pepper and salt to taste. When well blended, add the 2 tablespoons chicken stock or water. Cover the mixture and place in the refrigerator for at least 1 hour, preferably 2. In a large pot, bring the 1½ quarts of water to a boil. Add the bouillon cubes. Reduce the heat.

With wet hands, form eight balls and drop into the simmering water. Cover the pot and cook for a minimum of 45 minutes. The balls will expand as they cook. When they have achieved the desired softness, remove from the water with a slotted spoon.

If you are going to freeze the soup, let it cool, uncovered, before storing in the freezer—covering warm soup can cause it to ferment. Freeze matzo balls separately. After thawing frozen soup, add some fresh parsley and dill when reheating to revive those flavors.

To freeze matzo balls, place them on a flat pan or cookie sheet. Let cool, then cover with foil.

Serving Suggestions

1. Serve the soup with matzo balls only. (This soup also goes well with rice or egg noodles.
2. Before reheating the soup, return the chicken (on or off the bone), the matzo balls, and all the vegetables (except the onion) to the pot. Serve all together for a one-dish poached-chicken-in-the pot meal.
3. Serve the chicken and vegetables separately, either hot or at room temperature.

Serves 8

Black Bean Soup   Meat

> 1 cup black beans, washed
> 5 cups cold water
> 2 medium onions, coarsely chopped
> 1 clove garlic, coarsely chopped
> ¼ cup pareve margarine, melted
> ½ teaspoon curry powder
> ¼ teaspoon turmeric
> 2 medium potatoes, peeled and cut into quarters
> 2 medium carrots, quartered
> 2 parsnips, quartered
> 1 cup stewed tomatoes
> 1 10½-ounce can low-sodium kosher chicken broth
> 1 10½-ounce can low-sodium kosher beef broth

Soak the beans overnight. Drain. In 4 cups of cold water, cook the beans for approximately 1 hour or until soft. Set beans aside. In a large pot, sauté the onions and garlic in the margarine for about 5 minutes, until soft. Add 1 cup of cold water, the curry powder, turmeric, potatoes, carrots, and parsnips. Cook until the vegetables are soft. Add the stewed tomatoes and the beans. Put the mixture into a blender and purée. Pour the puréed vegetables back into the pot. Add the chicken and beef broths. Mix. Heat and serve.

Serves 8

APPETIZERS AND SALADS

Israeli Salad   Pareve

My grandfather, who was from Jaffa, Israel, introduced this salad to the family. It is still a Sunday morning breakfast tradition. It goes well with bagels, lox, and smoked fish and is equally delicious as a lunch, served in pita bread, or as a side dish with fried fish.

> Diced ripe tomato
> Diced green pepper
> Diced red pepper (optional)
> Diced cucumber
> Thinly sliced scallion
> Lettuce shredded into small pieces
> 1 tablespoon olive oil
> Salt and pepper to taste
> Fresh lemon

Mix the tomato, peppers, cucumber, scallion, and lettuce with the oil. Add salt and pepper to taste. Squeeze lemon juice on the salad to taste and toss. Serve at room temperature with lemon wedges on the side.

The exact proportions of tomatoes and other vegetables do not matter, although there should be proportionately more tomatoes.

Gerry's Hummus   Pareve

This is another Israeli dish, a snack food popular throughout the Middle East.

> 2 cups chickpeas, drained, liquid reserved
> 2 cloves garlic, crushed
> 1 tablespoon olive oil

1 teaspoon lemon juice
1 teaspoon salt
Paprika
Pita bread

Mix the chickpeas, garlic, oil, lemon juice, and salt in a blender. If the mixture is too thick, add a few tablespoons of the reserved chickpea liquid. Add more lemon juice to taste, if necessary. Place in a bowl, sprinkle paprika on top, and serve with warm pita bread wedges.

This dip can also be garnished with chopped parsley and olives.

Makes approximately 2½ cups.

Greek Salad   Pareve

1 large herring, sliced thin
1 large onion, sliced
2 tomatoes, diced
1 head cabbage, shredded
4 radishes, thinly sliced
1 cucumber, thinly sliced
2 carrots, peeled and thinly sliced
¼ cup olive oil
¼ cup vinegar
Salt and pepper to taste
¼ pound Greek olives

Mix all the ingredients except the olives together and marinate in the refrigerator overnight. Add the olives as garnish and serve.

Serves 4–6

Zena's Coleslaw, Cajun Style   Pareve

>   1 head cabbage, sliced or shredded
>   1 carrot, sliced
>   1 red pepper, chopped
>   1 small onion, diced
>   ½ cup white vinegar
>   1 teaspoon vegetable oil
>   1 teaspoon sugar
>   1 cup light mayonnaise
>   2 tablespoons sour cream
>   1–2 tablespoons Dijon mustard
>   ½–1 teaspoon chili powder
>   Parsley, dried or fresh, to taste
>   Salt and pepper to taste

Mix all the ingredients in a large bowl. Chill for 3 hours before serving.

Serves 12 as a side dish

Eggplant Au Claire   Pareve

>1 large eggplant, peeled and cubed
>½ cup plus 2 tablespoons olive oil
>2½ cups chopped onions
>1 cup chopped celery
>2 8-ounce cans plain tomato sauce
>¼ cup wine vinegar
>2 tablespoons sugar
>2 tablespoons capers, drained
>12 black olives, pitted
>Salt and pepper to taste

Sauté eggplant in ½ cup olive oil until lightly browned. Remove and set aside. Add the remaining olive oil to the pan and sauté the onions and celery until soft. Add the tomato sauce and simmer for 15 minutes. Add the eggplant and cook 15 minutes more. Add the vinegar, sugar, capers, olives, and salt and pepper to taste. Mash all the ingredients together. Serve with pita bread or crackers.

Serves 8–12 as an appetizer

PASTA AND NOODLES

Summer Pasta With Uncooked Tomato Sauce   Pareve

3 large, red vine-ripened tomatoes, skins removed
⅓ cup olive oil
4 medium garlic cloves, peeled and halved
1 clove garlic, chopped fine
¼ teaspoon or less red pepper flakes, to taste
½ cup coarsely torn fresh basil leaves
2 or 3 sprigs fresh Italian parsley, coarsely
    chopped (optional)
Salt and pepper to taste
Penne or other tubular-shaped paste such as rigatoni
    or ziti
Grated kosher Parmesan or Romano cheese (optional)

To remove their skins, place the tomatoes in a pot of boiling water for 15–20 seconds. Drain in a colander and pour cold water over them. They should then peel easily. Core the tomatoes and chop coarsely. Place the tomatoes and their liquid in a large bowl. Add the olive oil, the garlics, red pepper flakes, basil, parsley if desired, and salt and pepper to taste. Mix. Cover the bowl with a paper towel and let stand at room temperature for at least 4 hours, stirring, if possible, once or twice. (The mixture can also be put in the refrigerator overnight, but be sure to bring it to room temperature before serving.) Before serving, remove the large pieces of garlic from the sauce.

Cook and drain the pasta. Add the sauce and toss. Add cheese, if desired, and toss again. Serve in soup bowls, with toasted garlic bread to sop up the extra sauce.

Do *not* try this recipe with pale winter tomatoes found in the supermarket.

If cheese is added to this dish, it becomes a dairy, not pareve, meal.

Serves 3

Harry's Sweet Noodle Pudding (Kugel)   Dairy

Kugel is a traditional dish of the Ashkenazim or Yiddish-speaking Jews from Central or Eastern Europe. This thick, rich noodle pudding is often served at the Jewish New Year, Rosh Hashanah, when sweet foods are eaten to symbolize a sweet year to come.

> 3 eggs
> 1 12-ounce can evaporated milk
> ¾ cup sugar
> 1 teaspoon vanilla
> 1 16-ounce package wide egg noodles, cooked, drained, and cooled
> 1 pound cottage cheese
> Small box of raisins
> Cinnamon to taste
> ¼ pound butter

Preheat the oven to 350° F. Mix the eggs, evaporated milk, sugar, and vanilla. Add the noodles. Mix in the cottage cheese, raisins, and cinnamon. Melt the butter and add half of it to the noodle mixture. Pour the remaining butter into a lasagna-size baking pan and coat the pan. Pour in the noodle mixture and bake for 1 hour or until golden.

Serves 15–18

Kasha Varnishkes   Pareve

A traditional Russian dish, popular in the Ashkenazi cuisine.

> 1 egg
> 1 cup uncooked whole kasha (buckwheat groats)
> 2 cups boiling water
> 2 tablespoons oil
> 1 onion, diced
> 1 cup diced mushrooms (optional)
> 1½ cups cooked and drained bowtie egg noodles
> 1 cup steamed peas (optional)
> 1 teaspoon salt
> ¼ teaspoon pepper

In a large bowl, beat the egg. Add the kasha and mix until all the grains are coated with egg. Heat a saucepan or skillet and add the kasha-egg mixture, stirring until the kasha grains are dry. Pour the boiling water over the kasha, cover, and simmer until all the liquid is absorbed and kasha is dry and fluffy.

In another saucepan, heat the oil and sauté the onion and mushrooms, if desired, until onions are golden. Combine the bowties, kasha, onion and mushrooms, and steamed peas, if desired, and mix until all are combined. Add salt and pepper and serve.

Chicken bouillon can be substituted for the water, making this a meat dish.

Serves 4–6

POTATOES AND RICE

Sephardic Potatoes   Meat

Sephardi or Ladino (Judeo-Spanish) speaking Jews trace their ancestry back to medieval Iberia (Sepharad is the Hebrew name for Spain). When King Ferdinand and Queen Isabella expelled the Jews from their country in 1492, many found safe refuge in North Africa and the lands of the Ottoman Empire. As a result, Sephardic cuisine reflects a number of cultures of the Mediterranean and Middle East, including Greece, Turkey, Syria and Persia, as well as Spain and Portugal.

> 1 large Spanish onion, sliced
> 2 cloves garlic, minced
> ¼ cup olive oil
> 1 stick margarine
> 6 medium potatoes
> 3 large carrots, diced
> 2 tablespoons diced red pepper
> 2 tablespoons chopped parsley
> 1¼ teaspoons salt
> ¼ teaspoon pepper
> 1 can clear low-sodium kosher chicken broth

Sauté the onion and garlic in the olive oil and margarine until tender. Add the potatoes and carrots and sauté for 10 minutes. Add the remaining ingredients. Reduce the heat, cover, and simmer for 20 minutes, until the vegetables are soft.

Serves 8–10

Spicy Potato Rounds   Dairy

   8 medium baking potatoes, thinly sliced in rounds
   ½ teaspoon dry mustard
   ½ teaspoon paprika
   ¼ teaspoon chili powder
   2 small onions, peeled and minced
   ½ cup butter, melted

Preheat the oven to 425° F. Place the potatoes in a single layer on Teflon cookie sheets. Mix the spices and onions in the melted butter and drizzle over the potatoes. Bake for about 45 minutes or until the potatoes are golden.

   If you like really spicy foods, use hot paprika rather than sweet.

Serves 8

Herbed Potatoes   Dairy

> 4 large baking potatoes, unpared
> ¼ cup melted butter
> ¼ cup olive oil
> 3 medium cloves garlic, minced
> Salt to taste
> ½ teaspoon dried rosemary or dried thyme

Preheat the oven to 400° F. Cut the potatoes into ¼-inch-thick slices. Place overlapping slices in a buttered oven-to-table baking dish or glass pie plate. Mix the butter and oil and brush the slices with the mixture. Pour any remaining mixture over potatoes. Sprinkle with the garlic, salt, and rosemary or thyme. Bake for 25 to 30 minutes or until the potatoes are done and browned at the edges.

If pareve margarine is substituted for the butter, this recipe becomes pareve.

Serves 4

Baked Rice   Dairy

> 2½ tablespoons butter
> 2 tablespoon minced onion
> ½ teaspoon minced garlic
> 1 cup uncooked rice
> 1½ cups water
> 3 sprigs parsley
> 1 sprig fresh thyme or ¼ teaspoon dried
> Salt and pepper to taste
> ½ bay leaf

Preheat the oven to 400° F. Melt half the butter in a casserole and sauté the onion and garlic, stirring until the onion is translucent. Add the rice and blend over a low flame until the rice is coated. Stir in the water, making sure there are no lumps in the rice. Add the parsley, thyme, salt, pepper and bay leaf. Cover with a tight-fitting lid and bring to a boil. Remove the casserole from the flame and place in the oven. Bake for exactly 17 minutes (this is not an arbitrary number). After removing the casserole from the oven, discard the parsley, thyme sprig, and bay leaf. Stir in the remaining butter and serve.

If pareve margarine is substituted for the butter, the recipe becomes pareve.

Serves 4

VEGETABLES

Acorn Squash With Peas   Pareve

>1 large acorn squash
>1 tablespoon margarine (pareve)
>1 tablespoon brown sugar
>2 cups fresh or frozen peas
>Fresh mint leaves (optional)

Preheat the oven to 400° F. Cut the squash in half and scoop out
the seeds. If the bottoms are not flat, cut away a small portion so
the halves will stay upright. Dot the rim and center cavity of
each half with margarine and sprinkle with brown sugar. Place
on a baking sheet, cavity side up, and bake until fork-tender.
While the squash is baking, cook the peas (with mint, if desired).
When the squash is ready, fill the cavities with peas and serve.

Serves 2

Chip's Carrot Pudding   Dairy

>1 pound carrots, cooked and riced
>About ⅞ cup granulated brown sugar
>1⅔ cups canola oil
>3 eggs
>2 teaspoons baking powder
>½ cup Bisquick
>1 11-ounce can crushed pineapple

Preheat oven to 350° F. Mix all the ingredients together and pour
into a greased baking dish or pan. Bake for 1 hour. This freezes
well.

Serves 12

Florence's Vegetarian Cutlets   Pareve

    2 medium potatoes, cubed
    2 onions, one cubed, one coarsely chopped
    3 carrots, sliced
    ½ cup finely chopped celery
    ½ cup finely chopped green beans
    ½ cup peas
    1 egg
    ½ cup matzo meal
    Salt and pepper to taste
    ¼ cup vegetable oil

Boil a pot of water. Add the potatoes, the cubed onion, and the carrots and cook for 15 minutes. Add the celery, beans, and peas and cook another 15 minutes. Drain and place the mixture in a large chopping bowl. Add the chopped onion, then finely chop all the vegetables. Add the egg, matzo meal, and salt and pepper to taste. Mix. Cover and put in the refrigerator for ½ hour. Shape the mixture into six large patties and fry in the vegetable oil until browned on both sides. Drain on paper towels. These vegetable patties can be frozen.

Serves 6

Sandy's Holiday Cranberry Compote   Pareve

1 16-ounce can cranberry sauce (whole berry)
1 package frozen strawberries, drained
1 cup walnut pieces
2 8-ounce jars applesauce

Mix all but ½ cup of the walnut pieces in a large bowl. Refrigerate for a few hours so the flavors have time to blend. Add the remaining walnuts as garnish.

Serves 8

Lynn's Spinach Pie   Pareve

4 packages frozen chopped spinach, thawed and water
    squeezed out
2 eggs
4 tablespoons melted margarine
½ cup matzo meal
½ cup kosher nondairy creamer
Salt to taste

Preheat oven to 350° F. Mix all the ingredients together. Pour the mixture into an 8 × 10-inch greased baking pan. Bake for 1 hour, until the top is lightly browned and the spinach mixture is firm.

Serves 12

Joyce's Zucchini Soufflé   Dairy

> 3 large zucchini, unpeeled, grated (about 3 cups)
> 1 cup Bisquick
> 1 large onion, chopped
> 4 eggs or equivalent egg substitute
> Fresh parsley, chopped, or dried parsley flakes, to taste
> Pepper to taste
> ½ cup olive oil
> Large chunk of cheese, grated

Preheat the oven to 350° F. Mix all the ingredients together. Pour into a greased baking dish and bake for about 1 hour, until the top is brown and crusty.

Joyce uses part-skim Jarlsberg, but other cheeses will work as well.

Serves 10–12

MEAT

My Favorite Chili   Meat

    1 pound lean chopped kosher beef
    2 tablespoons vegetable oil
    2 large onions, finely chopped
    4 medium garlic cloves, finely chopped
    4 tablespoons red chili powder
    2 teaspoons celery salt
    ½ teaspoon cayenne
    2 teaspoons ground cumin
    1 teaspoon dried basil
    1 teaspoon salt
    2 16-ounce cans plum tomatoes
    2 small bay leaves
    6 cups water
    2 small cinnamon sticks
    4 whole cloves
    2 green bell peppers, cored, seeded,
       and coarsely chopped
    2 16-ounce cans kidney beans

Brown the beef in a skillet, draining off as much fat as possible. Set aside. In the same skillet, heat the oil. Add the onions and garlic and cook until the onion is translucent. Add the meat. Stir in the remaining ingredients up through the cloves. Bring to a boil, then lower the heat and simmer, uncovered, for 2½ hours, stirring occasionally. Stir in the green peppers and kidney beans and simmer, uncovered, ½ hour longer. Remove the cinnamon sticks, bay leaves, and, if possible, the cloves. Taste and adjust seasonings if necessary. Serve over baked potatoes or rice.

    This chili freezes well. Use hot, mild, or a combination of chili powder, according to how spicy you like your chili.

Serves 6

Grandma Molly's Mish Mosh   Meat

This recipe is over seventy years old and has been enjoyed by three generations of my family. It was first served by my grandmother, who passed the recipe on to my mother and aunt, who then served it to their children. I always think of it as "comfort" food; it's a wonderful, simple one-dish meal for a cold winter night. "Mish Mosh" refers to the way the kids in my family always eat this dish, mashing the meat and potatoes together.

> 1 pound lean ground kosher beef
> Salt and pepper to taste
> 2 medium onions, coarsely chopped
> 2 medium carrots, cut into 1-inch chunks
> 4–5 medium potatoes, cut into thick slices
> 1 cup steamed green peas (optional)

Season the beef with salt and pepper and form into little balls—about 1½ to 2 inches in diameter. Bring a pot of water to a boil. Add the onions. Drop in the meatballs and bring the water to a boil again. Cover, reduce the heat, and cook for 10 minutes. Add the carrots and potatoes and cook until they are tender. Remove some of the liquid and set aside. Drain, add peas if desired, and serve in large bowls. Pour a spoonful or so of the reserved liquid over each dish. Good accompaniments for Mish Mosh are rye bread and sour pickles.

Serves 4

Meat and Vegetable Stew   Meat

> 1½ pounds ground kosher beef
> 1 tablespoon oil
> 1 large onion, chopped (makes 1 cup)
> 1 can condensed beef broth
> 1¼ cups water
> Dash of cayenne
> 1 bay leaf
> 6 medium potatoes, pared and quartered
> 1 tablespoon flour
> 2 green peppers, seeded, and chopped (or 1 green and 1
>   red pepper)
> 1 1-pound can tomatoes
> ¼ cup sliced green olives stuffed with pimientos
> Salt and pepper to taste

Shape the beef into 24 meatballs. Brown 12 at a time in a Teflon pot or one sprayed with kosher pan coating. Remove and set aside. Add the oil to the pot and sauté the onions until soft. Add the beef broth, 1 cup water, cayenne, and bay leaf. Return the meatballs to the pot. Cover, lower the heat, and simmer for 10 minutes. Add the potatoes. Simmer for 20 minutes, or until potatoes are tender. Remove the meatballs and potatoes with a slotted spoon. Remove and discard the bay leaf. Combine the flour and remaining ¼ cup water in a cup, then stir the mixture into the cooking liquid. Cook, stirring, until thickened. Return the meatballs and potatoes to the pot. Add the peppers, tomatoes, and olives. Lower the heat, cover, and simmer for 5 minutes. Add salt and pepper to taste.

Serves 6

Pot Roast With Lemon and Orange   Meat

    1 cup chopped onions
    3–5 garlic cloves, minced
    ½ cup olive oil
    3–4 pound kosher chuck roast, center cut, or brisket, as
        much fat removed as possible
    1 1-pound, 13-ounce can Italian tomatoes, drained
    1 15-ounce can tomato sauce
    1 orange, sliced as thinly as possible
    1 lemon, sliced as thinly as possible
    ½–1 pound small button mushrooms, cooked

Preheat the oven to 350° F. In a large roasting pan on top of the stove, brown the onions and garlic in the olive oil. Add the beef and brown quickly on all sides. Add the other ingredients, placing the orange and lemon slices on top of the meat. Cover, place in the oven, and bake until the meat is soft and tender, about 2 hours.

If fresh mushrooms are not available, canned mushrooms are okay.

Serves 6

FISH

Portuguese Fish Bundles   Pareve

> For each 1-serving bundle:
>   3 slices onion
>   1 bay leaf, broken into piece
>   1 4-ounce fillet of flounder, sole, fluke, or similar fish
>   3 slices peeled vine-ripe tomatoes
>   Dried oregano, to taste
>   Minced garlic, to taste
>   Salt and pepper to taste
>   1 tablespoon dry red wine

Preheat the oven to 350° F. To make each bundle, use a square of aluminum foil, large enough to seal packet loosely around fish, shiny side up. Spray it lightly with cooking spray. Place the onion slices and bay leaf pieces in the center of the foil. Place the fish fillet on top, and cover with the tomato slices. Sprinkle lightly with oregano, garlic, salt, and pepper to taste. Add the wine. Fold the foil loosely over the fish, crimping the edges so that the liquid will not leak out. Place bundles directly on an oven rack and cook undisturbed for ½ hour.

See the recipe for Summer Pasta, page 82, for directions on removing tomato skins.

Mustard Dilled Salmon

Pareve

> 4 salmon steaks, about 1¼-inch thick
> Salt and pepper to taste
> 2 tablespoons olive oil
> 2 tablespoons lemon juice
> 1 teaspoon Dijon mustard
> 3 tablespoons minced fresh dill

Season the salmon with salt and pepper and place in a glass or ceramic dish. Combine all the other ingredients and pour over the fish. Marinate in the refrigerator for at least 1 hour, turning the steaks a few times so that both sides are covered with the marinade. The salmon can then be broiled or grilled on each side until cooked through.

Serves 4

CHICKEN

Herbed Chicken Rolls Stuffed With Mushrooms

Meat

6 kosher chicken cutlets
Salt and pepper to taste
2 egg whites
Unseasoned bread crumbs
⅓ cup corn or canola oil
¼ teaspoon dried rosemary
¼ teaspoon dried sage
2 teaspoons chopped fresh parsley
½ cup dry white wine

Filling

10 ounces fresh mushrooms, chopped
2 tablespoons corn or canola oil
¼ teaspoon salt
A few tablespoons unseasoned bread crumbs

Preheat the oven to 350° F.

To make the filling, sauté the chopped mushrooms in the oil until they are soft, about 8–10 minutes. Stir in the salt. Add bread crumbs to absorb any liquid and to bind the mixture.

Season the chicken cutlets on both sides with salt and pepper to taste. Place 1 to 2 tablespoons of filling on each cutlet and roll up. Secure with a toothpick. Dip each rolled cutlet in egg white and then in bread crumbs. Place in a greased shallow baking pan. Mix the oil, rosemary, sage and parsley and pour over the chicken rolls. Place in the oven and bake uncovered for about 25 minutes. Pour the wine over the chicken and bake another 15 minutes, basting several times with the sauce.

Serves 4–6

Orange Tarragon Chicken   Meat

> 1 cup orange juice
> 2 tablespoons low-salt soy sauce
> 8 pieces kosher chicken, skin removed
> 1 cup unseasoned bread crumbs
> 2 tablespoons tarragon
> ½ teaspoon black pepper
> 3 tablespoons corn or canola oil
> 2 onions, sliced
> 10 ounces fresh mushrooms, sliced
> 1 can undiluted kosher chicken soup
> ½ to 1 cup white wine

Preheat the oven to 375° F. Mix the orange juice and soy sauce and then marinate the chicken parts for 15 minutes. Combine the bread crumbs, tarragon, and black pepper and coat the chicken pieces with the mixture. Fry the chicken in the oil until both sides are browned. Remove and place in a baking dish. In the same pan, brown the onions and mushrooms, then pour them over the chicken. Mix the chicken soup and wine and pour over the chicken. Cover with aluminum foil and bake in the oven for ¾ hour.

Serves 4–6

Crispy Oven-Baked Lemon Ginger
Sesame Chicken   Meat

⅔ cup lemon juice

⅓ cup light brown sugar

3 tablespoons corn or canola oil

1 teaspoon ground ginger or 2 teaspoons slivered fresh

¼ teaspoon dry mustard

2 kosher broiler/fryer chickens, about 2½ pounds each,
    cut up and with skin removed

1⅓ cups matzo meal

½ cup sesame seeds

1 teaspoon paprika

In a large bowl, combine the lemon juice, brown sugar, oil, ginger, and mustard. Add the chicken pieces and toss until coated. Cover and refrigerate for several hours to marinate, turning the pieces occasionally.

Preheat the oven to 400° F. Line two roasting pans with aluminum foil, covered with a wire rack.

In a plastic bag, combine the matzo meal, sesame seeds, and paprika. Shake the chicken pieces, a few at a time, in the crumb mixture. Place the pieces on the racks in the roasting pans and bake in the oven for approximately 50 minutes, until the chicken is tender. Serve hot or cold.

Serves 8

COOKIES

Mandelbrot   Pareve

The literal translation of mandelbrot is "almond bread." This twice-baked Eastern European cookie bears a strong resemblance to Italian biscotti. If chocolate chips are used, the recipe becomes dairy.

2¼ cups unsifted flour
¾ cup sugar
Pinch of salt
½ teaspoon baking powder
½ cup corn or canola oil
3 eggs
1 teaspoon vanilla
½ cup sliced almonds or ¼ cup sliced almonds and ¼ cup chocolate chips

Preheat the oven to 375° F. Grease a cookie sheet. Combine the flour, sugar, salt, and baking powder. Make a hole in the middle of the mixture and add the oil, eggs, and vanilla. Stir until mixed, then stir in the almonds or almonds and chocolates. With floured hands, form the dough into three long loaves. Place on the cookie sheet and bake in the oven for ½ hour (the loaves should be brown on top). Remove from the oven.

While the loaves are still hot, cut them on an angle into slices ½ to 1 inch thick. Lay the pieces flat on the cookie sheet. Return to the oven and bake until the tops are browned, about 5–10 minutes. Turn the pieces over to brown on the other side if necessary.

Because these cookies are twice baked, they will stay fresh for two weeks if kept in a tightly covered container. If they lose their crispness, reheat them in a 375° F. oven for 5–10 minutes on each side.

Makes 36 cookies

Maren's Meringues   Dairy

This easy recipe is fun to make with children.

>   2 egg whites
>   ½ teaspoon peppermint extract or ½ teaspoon vanilla
>   Dash of salt
>   ⅛ teaspoon cream of tartar
>   ¾ cup sugar (or less if you like your meringues less
>   sweet)
>   ½ cup chocolate bits

Preheat the oven to 325° F. Line a cookie sheet with plain brown paper. Combine the egg whites, extract, salt, and cream of tartar and beat until peaks form. Gradually add the sugar, beating until stiff. Fold in the chocolate bits. Drop by teaspoonfuls on the cookie sheet, 1 to 2 inches apart. Bake in the oven for 20–25 minutes. Remove from the paper when cool.

Makes approximately 2 dozen 2–inch meringues

Rugalach   Dairy

> 1 cup unsalted butter, softened
> ½ pound cream cheese, softened
> 2 cups all-purpose flour, sifted
> 1 cup walnuts, finely chopped
> ½ cup raisins
> ½ cup sugar
> 1½ teaspoons cinnamon

Cream the butter and cream cheese together in a large bowl. Mix in the flour until it is all incorporated. Knead gently if necessary. Refrigerate for 2 hours.

Form the dough into 10–14 balls. Roll each ball out into a 6-inch circle. If dough is sticky, dust it with a bit of flour. With a sharp knife or pastry wheel, cut each pastry into quarters.

Preheat the oven to 350° F. Combine the walnuts, raisins, sugar, and cinnamon and place a teaspoonful of the mixture into the center of each quarter. Spread the mixture to cover the dough. Beginning at the wide edge of the quarter, roll the dough up toward the point. Place on an ungreased cookie sheet and bake in the oven for approximately 15–20 minutes or until golden brown.

For a variation, use 1 cup chocolate bits instead of the walnuts, raisins, cinnamon, and sugar.

Makes 40–56 cookies

CHAPTER TEN

KOSHER SOURCES

These directories are by no means an all-inclusive list of kosher establishments and services, nor do they constitute an endorsement of any product or service by the author or publisher, or an endorsement of the reliability of the kosher certification. Readers should also be advised that the kosher status of hotels, restaurants, markets, and products—and their addresses and telephone numbers—can change. If readers have any questions about the kosher status of a particular listing, they should contact the certifying agency or speak with a local rabbi.

The author would be interested in hearing from readers about changes in kosher certification that they encounter, as well as information about new kosher establishments and services in their cities. She can be reached in care of Carol Publishing Group, 120 Enterprise Ave., Secaucus, NJ 07094.

HOTELS, RESORTS, TRAVEL AGENTS, AND TOUR GUIDES

FLORIDA

Catalina Inn Hotel Kosher Resorts
I-4 Exit 32 & John Young Pkwy.
Orlando
800-747-0013, 407-238-9968

Crown Hotel & Beach Club
4041 Collins Ave.
Miami Beach
800-327-8163, 305-531-5771

Four Points Sheraton
Collins Avenue & 43rd St.
Miami Beach
888-494-3424

Jupiter Beach Resort
5 N. A1A at Indiantown Rd.
Jupiter Beach (West Palm Beach)
800-749-4300, 954-974-0777

Lucerne Hotel
Boardwalk at 41st St. & Collins Ave.
Miami Beach
800-833-0462

Sans Souci Spa & Resort
Boardwalk at 32nd St.
Miami Beach
800-327-8470, 305-672-4129

Sasson Hotel Ocean Resort
2001 Collins Ave.
Miami Beach
800-327-7111

Saxony Hotel
3201 Collins Ave.
Miami Beach
800-327-8169

Versailles Hotel
Boardwalk at 34th St. & Collins Ave.
Miami Beach
800-833-0462, 305-672-4233

MASSACHUSETTS

Lilac Inn Bed & Breakfast
Lenox (the Berkshires)
413-637-2172

NEW HAMPSHIRE

Arlington Hotel
Bethlehem
603-869-3353

NEW JERSEY

Seasons Resort
Great Gorge
800-742-8742

NEW YORK

Best Western Paramount
Parksville (Catskills)
800-922-4398

Chalet Hotel
Woodbourne (Catskills)
718-338-8653, 718-637-3450

Concord Hotel
Kiamesha Lake (Catskills)
800-431-3850, 914-794-4000

Davidman's Homowack
Spring Glen (Catskills)
800-243-4567

Fallsview
Ellenville (Catskills)
800-822-8439

Golden Acres Farm & Ranch
Family Resort
Cooperstown
800-252-7787

Kutsher's
Monticello (Catskills)
800-431-1273, 914-794-6000

Levine's Washington Hotel
Beach 125th St. & Rockaway,
Beach Blvd.,
Belle Harbor
718-634-4244, 718-474-9671

Oppenheimer's Regis Hotel
Fleischmann's, NY (Catskills)
800-468-3598

Pine's
South Fallsburg (Catskills)
800-36-PINES
(Kosher & nonkosher dining
rooms)

Raleigh Hotel
South Fallsburg (Catskills)
800-446-4003

Tamarack Lodge
Between Ellenville & Woodbourne
(Catskills)
800-732-2715, 914-647-3500

PENNSYLVANIA

Mt. Airy Lodge & Resort
Mt. Pocono
717-839-8811

RHODE ISLAND

Hotel Viking
Newport
401-847-3300

VIRGINIA

The Kosher Hotel of Virginia
Richmond
800-733-8474, 804-740-2000

FRANCE

Lebrun Hotel
4 Rue Lamartine
Paris
48-78-75-52

MEXICO

Hyatt Regency Alcupulco
800-233-1234

SWITZERLAND

Levin's Hotel Metropole
Arosa
0011-4181-377-4444

The following travel agents and tour guides specialize in domestic &/or foreign kosher tours or kosher holiday packages.

Dynamo Dave's Discovery Tours
85-30 121st St.
Kew Gardens, NY 11415
800-646-9260, 718-847-4698
(Biking, kayaking, and boating Tours of Florida, New York, New England)

Elite Dimensions Tours
(Passover season only)
718-268-8080
outside NY: 800-228-4525
Fax: 718-268-4638

Kesher Kosher Tours
370 Lexington Ave
NY, NY 10017
212-949-9580
outside NY: 800-847-0700

Lasko Family Kosher Tours
2699 Stirling Rd, Suite C-405
Ft. Lauderdale, FL 33312
800-532-9119, 954-894-6000
Fax: 954-894-0993

Leisure Time Tours
145-98 Brewer Blvd.
Queens, NY 11434
(Passover season only)
718-528-0700
outside NY: 800-223-2624
Fax. 718-527-8676

Mendy Vim's Holidays & Vacations
(Passover season only)
718-998-4477
outside NY: 800-464-VIMS

Presidential Kosher Holidays
(Passover season only)
718-332-3900
outside NY: 800-950-1240

Richnik's Ltd.
362 W. 23rd St.
NY, NY 10011
(Foreign & domestic vacations)
212-807-0500
Fax: 212-645-7347

Scandinavian Trio Tours
626 Montgomery St.
Brooklyn, NY 11225
(Guided tours to Scandinavia & Spain)
718-773-0440
Fax: 718-771-4565

Sunburst Kosher Tours
1555 E. 19th St.
Brooklyn, NY 11230
(Domestic package tours for groups & individuals)
718-339-0091
outside NY: 800-484-7245
Code 5683

Touring Friends, Ltd.
P.O. Box 159
Lawrence, NY 11559
(Foreign & domestic group tours)
718-471-6459, 718-686-0580
Fax: 718-471 6582, 718-868-0587

Universal Kosher Tours Ltd
119 N. Park Ave.
Rockville Centre, NY 11570
(Passover season only)
516-766-5140, 800-221-2791,

About Food

Some resort hotels that do not have their own kosher dining rooms can make arrangements for kosher meals to be served to guests. (Note: A number of resort hotels are host to special "Kosher for Passover" package tours.) Check with your travel agent or the hotel when booking rooms.

Another option might be "My Own Meals," a line of vacuum-packed kosher meals available in dairy, meat, and pareve dishes. They come with their own disposable warming devices and are packaged in small, compact boxes that fit easily into luggage. For further information on "My Own Meals" contact: See-Me Travel, 24 Dr. Frank Rd., Spring Valley, NY 10977 914-426-1425, Fax: 914-426-1425.

Airline Food

All U.S. airline carriers will provide kosher meals to passengers as long as they are given advance notice (at least 24 hours) that such meals are wanted. Three million prepackaged kosher meals are served on U.S. airlines each year.

All airline meal services are contracted out to large food-service caterers, which are also responsible for other special-request meals such as vegetarian, lactose-intolerant, and salt-free diets, as well as kosher.

Generally, airline food is not prepared fresh at an airport kitchen, but is brought in frozen. On some flights the food is cooked on board; other flights serve preheated food. Cold kosher meals come sealed in plastic; hot kosher meals are double-sealed.

An exception is the meals served on El Al, Israel's national airline, on international flights from New York's JFK Airport. They are prepared fresh at the airline's airport commissary, which is certified kosher.

Benson's Gourmet Seasonings
800-325-5619
Kosher all-natural, salt-free, sugar-free, preservative-free, MSG-free seasonings. Free catalog.

Broadway Basketeers
For brochure or custom orders:
888-599-GIFT, 24 hrs.
Gift baskets. Ships throughout U.S. & Canada. Free color brochure.
To order: 800-378-7173

Chocolate Emporium
888-246-2528
Chocolates and confections. Free catalog.

The Creative Basket
718-380-4326
Food & gift baskets; delivery throughout U.S.

Delancey Street Dessert Company
New York City
212-254-0977, 800-254-5254
Babkas, rugalach, mandelbrot, and other baked goods; also sugar-free products. Free catalog.

Fairytale Brownies
Scottsdale, Arizona
800-324-7982
Belgian chocolate brownies. Free catalog.

Freeda Vitamins
800-777-3737
Kosher vitamins contain no sugar, starch, sulfates, salt filler, coal tar dyes, or animal stearates. Free catalog.

Global Products & Distribution
2480 Briarcliff Rd., Ste. 285
Atlanta, GA 30329
800-435-1755, Fax: 404-325-7802
Holiday gift baskets. Ships throughout United States and to Israel.

Godiva Chocolatier
800-9GODIVA, (946-3482), 8 A.M.–11 P.M. EST, 7 days a wk. Internet: www.godiva.com, AOL keyword: godiva
Chocolate gift boxes and baskets. Most Godiva products are kosher and are so indicated in their catalog. Catalog available.

GoodEats
P.O. Box 756
Richboro, PA 18954
800-490-0044, 215-674-2117, M-F 8:30 A.M.–6:00 P.M. EST
Fax: 215-443-7087, E-mail: good-eats@voicenet.com
Natural foods, health & beauty supplies, pet food, kitchenware &

home care products, organic clothing, books & magazines; over 2,000 items available. Specializes in organic, kosher, macrobiotic, environment-friendly, and cruelty-free products. Catalog $3.00; refundable with first purchase.

Hamakor Judaica
"The Source for Everything Jewish"
P.O. Box 48836
Niles, IL 60714
800-426-2567, 24 hrs., Fax: 847-966-4033
Kosher snack foods, chocolates, delicatessen, gift baskets, cookbooks. Free catalog. Online catalog available at http://www.jewish-source.com.

H&H Bagels
639 W 46th St.
2239 Broadway
New York City
212-595-8000
Open 24 hrs.; ships worldwide.

Herman Glick's Sons Kosher Food Emporium
100-15 Queens Blvd.
Forest Hills, New York
800-GLICKSS, 718-896-7736
Meat and nonperishable items.

Kosher Connections
3195 SW. Raleighview Dr.
Portland, Oregon
800-950-7227
Kosher gourmet foods from the Pacific Northwest and Israel: willow gift baskets, alder-smoked salmon, fresh berry preserves, dried Oregon cherries, chocolates, low-fat delicacies. Ships to U.S. & Canada. Illustrated brochure and price list.

Kosher Cornucopia/Gifts Direct
Box 326, Beechwood Rd.
Jeffersonville, NY 12748
800-756-7437
Gift baskets and gourmet foods, including smoked salmon, smoked trout, dried salami, knishes, candies, chocolates, popcorn, fruit, nuts. Ships throughout U.S. & to Canada & Israel. Free catalog.

Kosher Delight
212-541-GIFT
Kosher delicacies: hand-dipped chocolates, Alaskan smoked salmon, gourmet coffee, nuts, candy, baked goods, cider.

Kosher Maven
800-229-2677, 413-436-0506
Gift baskets, including fruits, nuts, chocolates, pasta & sauces; some products fat-free, sugar-free.

Long Island Kosher Meat & Poultry
829 W 181st St.
New York City
212-795-0248
Fresh & frozen meat; delivery throughout U.S.

Maxi-Health Research
800-544-MAXI, 718-645-2222
Vitamins and supplements.

Meals on Wings
888-426-MEAL
Web site: www.koshermealon-wings.com
Fresh-frozen custom dinners ready for oven or microwave. Overnight delivery available.

Mr. Kosher Global Shopping
Fax: 860-523-5988, E-mail: kosher@mrkosher.com
Gourmet foods, bakery items, delicatessen, meat.

Musicon Deer Farms
Goshen, New York
914-294-6378
Freshly frozen kosher venison
raised free of hormones, steroids,
chemicals, and additives. Ships
individually wrapped butchered
cuts throughout U.S. Call for price
list & recipes.

N.Y. Flying Pizza Pies
c/o Broadway's Jerusalem 2
1375 Broadway
New York, NY 10018
800-969-6974, 212-398-1475
Fax: 212-398-6797, Online:
www.flyingpizzas.com
Fresh kosher pizza; ships throughout U.S.

Oneg Catering
Brooklyn, New York
718-438-3388, Fax: 718-438-5135
Fresh-frozen packaged kosher
meals shipped overnight via
Federal Express. Shipment available throughout U.S. & to Puerto
Rico & surrounding islands. Menu
available.

Penn Street Coffee Cake
800-842-2537, Online:
http://pennstreet.com
Coffee cakes in 8 flavors; ships
everywhere. Catalog.

Pepperidge Farm Holiday Gift
Collection
P.O. Box 917
Clinton, CT 06413-0917
800-243-9314, 8 A.M.–11 P.M. EST, 7
days a wk
Baked goods, cookies, brownies,
chocolates, candies, gift baskets &
decorated tins. Catalog available. A
number of products are kosher and
are so labeled in catalog.

Platters for All Occasions
800-9-PLATER
Dried fruit, nuts, candy; ships
throughout U.S.

Sarabeth's Kitchen
2291 Second Ave,
New York, NY 10035
800-PRESERVE
Naturally flavored, preservative-
free preserves, including orange-
apricot marmalade, cherry-plum
preserve, strawberry-peach preserve, peach-apricot preserve, apri-
cot-pineapple-currents preserve.
Free catalog.

Second Avenue Deli by Mail
156 Second Ave.
New York, NY 10003
800-692-3354
In NY call 212-677-0606
Online: www.quicklink.com/
-NYdeli
Kosher salamis and other deli
items; rugalach. Ships anywhere in
U.S. Free color catalog.

Shaklee Food Supplements
888-8SHKLEE
Kosher vitamins; natural personal-
care products. Free delivery
throughout continental U.S.
Catalog $2.00.

Start Fresh Weight Control
Program
4813 12th Ave.
Brooklyn, NY 11219
800-226-5000, 718-851-0081, Fax:
718-851-4192
Kosher diet foods low in fat, calories, sodium. Ships anywhere in
U.S. Free brochure.

Sugar Plum
800-44-SUGAR (447-8427)
Chocolates, gifts.

To Life Food & Herbs
220 Southwest Freeway, Ste. 400
Houston, TX 77098
800-317-3449, 713-771-5366
9 A.M.–5 P.M. CST, M–F
Fax: 713-771-6065, Web site:
mweiss@onramp.net
All kosher products: organic foods,
health food & related items, flour,
candy, cereal, milk, beans, grains,
tofu, pastas, salad dressings, condiments, cooking oils, tea; Oriental
gourmet items, sushi nori sheets,
wasabi, mirin, Umeboshi plums,
Thai peanut sauce, soba noodles,
brown rice vinegar, sesame oils;
vitamins and supplements. Ships
anywhere in U.S. Free catalog.

The Well-Bread Loaf
Congers, NY 10920
800-937-9252
Brownies, baked goods. Free
brochure.

Wolsk's Gourmet Confectioners
81 Ludlow St.
New York, NY 10002
212-475-0704, Fax: 212-673-2233

Gift baskets, dried fruit, nuts,
hand-dipped chocolates, international candies, coffees, teas, fresh
baked goods; sugar-free & low-
calorie items available. Ships
nationwide.

Zabar's
2245 Broadway
New York, NY 10024
212-787-2000, Fax: 212-580-4477
E-mail:infor@zabars.com
One of New York City's largest and
best-known gourmet markets. A
wide selection of gourmet kosher
items, including baked goods, coffees, smoked salmon. Catalog
available.

Zaro's Bread Basket
800-624-8559, 212-292-0175
E-mail: zaro@nybagels.com,
Internet: http://www.
nybagels.com
Baked goods. Ships throughout
U.S. Free catalog.

RESTAURANTS AND CATERERS*

Note: Many hotels in large metropolitan areas either maintain separate kosher kitchens or can have their kitchens koshered for kosher caterers. A number of those hotels are listed in this directory.

---

*Indicates a restaurant that also does catering.

ARIZONA

Phoenix

JJ's Fine Kosher Foods & Catering
1331 E. Northern Ave.
602-997-5555

Laura's Kitchen
4818 N. 7th St.
602-263-9377

CALIFORNIA

Los Angeles

Ashrafi Restaurant
1422 Westwood Blvd.
310-234-9191

Aviv Catering
310-278-1581

The Beverly Grand Hotel,
7257 Beverly Blvd.
213-939-1633,
Has a kosher kitchen for caterers.

Beverly Hills Caterers
310-330-7700

Beverly Hills Cuisine
9025 Wilshire Blvd.
310-247-1239

Caterering by Brenda
310-203-8365

Chana's Cuisine Catering
310-659-2834

Chick 'N Chow Chinese Food
9301 W. Pico Blvd.
310-274-5595

Cohen's Restaurant
316 E. Pico Blvd.
213-742-8888

Dizengoff Restaurant
8103½ Beverly Blvd.
213-651-4465

Elat Burger
9340 W. Pico Blvd.
310-278-4692

Elegant Caterers
9030 W. Olympic Blvd.
310-274-8856

Elite Cuisine
7119 Beverly Blvd.
213-930-1303

Falafel Village
16060 Ventura Blvd.
818-783-1012

Fish Grill
7226 Beverly Blvd.
213-937-7162

Fishing Well*
8975 W. Pico Blvd.
310-859-9429

Glatt Hut*
9303 W. Pico Blvd.
310-246-1900

Golan Restaurant
13075 Victory Blvd.
818-989-5423

Grill Express Restaurant
501 N. Fairfax Ave.
213-655-0649

Ha-Baguette Restaurant
8859 W. Pico Blvd.
310-247-1165

Hadar*
12514 Burbank Blvd.
818-762-1155
Chinese/Ethiopian

Harry & Rena Drexler's Restaurant
12519-½ Burbank Blvd.
818-761-6405

I'm a Deli & Restaurant
8930 W. Pico Blvd.
310-274-2452

Judy's*
129 N. La Brea
213-934-7667

Kabob & Chinese Food
9180 W. Pico Blvd.
310-274-4007

La Glatt
446 N. Fairfax Ave.
213-658-7730

La Gondola Ristorante Italiano
6405 Wilshire Blvd.
213-852-1915

Lax Catering
213-934-1638

Le Chaim Catering
213-654-2443

Magic Carpet Restaurant
8566 W. Pico Blvd.
310-652-8507

Micheline's Catering
310-204-5334

Milk N' Honey
8837 W. Pico Blvd.
310-858-8850

Milky Way
9108 W. Pico Blvd.
310-859-0004

Mosaique Restaurant
8164 W. 3rd St.
213-951-1133

Nagile Pizza
9016 W. Pico Blvd.
310-550-7735

Nessim's*
8939 W. Pico Blvd.
310-859-9429

Olé
7912 Beverly Blvd.
213-933-7254
Tex-Mex

Orly Restaurant
12454 Magnolia Blvd.,
Valley Village
818-508-5570

Pasta Express
9340 W. Pico Blvd.
310-247-1131

Pat's
9233 W. Pico Blvd.
310-205-8705

Pico Deli
8826 W. Pico Blvd.
310-273-9381

Pizza Delight
435 N. Fairfax Ave.
213-655-7800

Pizza World
365 S. Fairfax Ave.
213-653-2896

Rimini Restaurant
9400 W. Olympic Blvd.
310-552-1056

Shalom Pizza
8715 W. Pico Blvd.
310-271-2255

Sharon's*
18608-½ Ventura Blvd.
818-344-7474

Simon's Catering
213-961-7271

Simon's La Glatt*
446 N. Fairfax Ave.
213-658-7730

Sinai Catering
12233 Santa Monica Blvd.
310-820-0048

Tiberias Restaurant
18046 Ventura Blvd., Encino
818-343-3705

Yummy Pita
1437 S. Robertson Blvd.
310-557-2122

Oakland

Holyland Restaurant
677 Rand St.
510-272-0535

San Diego

Eva's Fresh & Natural
6717 El Cajun Blvd.
619-462-5018
Vegetarian

Lang's Loaf
6165 El Cajun Blvd.
619-287-7306

Mossarella's Pizza
6366 El Cajun Blvd.
619-583-1636

San Francisco

Lotus Garden Vegetarian Chinese
Restaurant
532 Grant Ave.
415-397-0707

Sabra
419 Grant Ave.
415-982-3656

Stella's Pastry Cafe
446 Columbus St.
415-986-2914

This Is It
430 Geary St.
415-749-0201
Israeli cuisine

COLORADO

Denver

East Side Kosher Deli
5475 Leetsdale Dr.
303-322-9862

Elegance by Andrew
745 Quebec St.
303-388-8883

Mediterranean Health Cafe
2817 East 3rd Ave.
303-399-2940

CONNECTICUT

Bridgeport

Brooklawn Pizza
1718 Capitol Ave.
203-384-0504

Hartford

Sam & Jack's Deli
2471 Albany Ave.
860-570-1518

New Haven

Claire's Corner Copia
1000 Chapel St.
203-562-3888

Edge of the Woods
379 Whalley Ave.
203-782-1055

Stamford

Abel Caterers
800-942-2235

DISTRICT OF COLUMBIA

Kafe Katz
4850 Boiling Brook Pkwy.
Rockville, Maryland
301-468-0400

Kosher Express
5065 Nicholson Lane
Rockville, Maryland
301-770-1919

Max's Kosher Cafe
2307 University Blvd. W.
Wheaton, Maryland
301-946-6500

The Nut House
11419 Georgia Ave.
Wheaton, Maryland
301-942-5900

O'Fishel's*
2300 H St. NW
Washington, D.C.
202-452-1160

Royal Dragon
4830 Boiling Brook Pkwy.
Rockville, Maryland
301-468-1922

The following Washington area hotels maintain separate kosher kitchens for group reservations and catered events: Capital Hilton, 16th & K Sts. NW, 202-393-1000; Washington Hilton & Towers, 1919 Connecticut Ave. NW, 202-483-3000; Grand Hyatt, 1000 H St. NW, 202-582-1234; Park Hyatt, 24th & M Sts. NW, 202-789-1234; Holiday Inn Bethesda, 8120 Wisconsin Ave. Bethesda, Maryland, 301-352-4525; Fairview Park Marriott, 3111 Fairview Park Dr., Falls Church, Virginia, 703-849-0730; Washington Renaissance, 999 9th St. NW, 202-898-9000; Stouffer Renaissance Mayflower, 1127 Connecticut Ave. NW, 202-347-3000; Sheraton Washington, 2600 Woodley Rd. NW, 202-328-2000.

FLORIDA

Boca Raton

Deli Maven
8208 Glades Rd.
407-477-7008

Eilat Cafe
7158 N. Beracasa Way
407-368-6880

Falafel Armon
22767 U.S. Hwy. 441
407-477-0633

Miami Beach

Bagel Time Restaurant
3915 Alton Rd.
Miami Beach
305-538-0300

China Kikar Tel-Aviv
(inside Carriage Club)
5005 Collins Ave.
Miami Beach
305-866-3316

David's Glatt Kosher Deli
1790 NE. Miami Gardens, Miami

Embassy 41 Kosher Steak House*
1501 N. Miami Beach Blvd.
North Miami Beach
305-947-0037

Embassy Peking Tower Suite
4101 Pinetree Dr.
305-538-7550

Galleria Restaurant
(in Versailles Hotel)
34th St. & Collins Ave.
305-672-4233

Isaac's Kosher Kitchen*
16460 NE 16th Ave.
North Miami Beach
305-944-5222

Jerusalem Peking
(inside Days Inn)
4299 Collins Ave.
305-532-2263

Jerusalem Pizza
761 NE 167th St.
North Miami Beach
305-653-6662

Kosher Magic Caterers
1839 NE. 183rd St.
North Miami Beach
305-932-6687

Kosher Treats
1678 NE 164th St.
North Miami Beach
305-947-1800

Kosher World Take-Out
514 41st St.
305-532-2210

Miami Pita
175 Sunny Isles Blvd.
North Miami Beach
305-940-4007

Pinati Restaurant
2520 NE 186th St.
Miami Garden Drive
North Miami Beach
305-931-8086

Pineapple's Natural Health Food
Restaurant
530 41st St.
305-523-9731

Royal Hungarian Kosher
Restaurant
3425 Collins Ave.
305-532-8566

Sara's Natural Food Restaurant &
Kosher Kitchen
2214 NE. 123rd St.
North Miami Beach
305-891-3312

Sara's of Hollywood
3944 N. 46th Ave., Hollywood

Sara's Pizza
1127 NE 163rd St.
North Miami Beach

Shimmy's Pizza
514 41st St.

Skyline Grill
976 41st St.

South Beach Pita
1448 Washington Ave.
305-534-3706

Terrace Oceanside Restaurant
1960 S. Ocean Dr., Hallandale
954-454-9444

Wing Wang II
1640 NE 164th St.
North Miami Beach
305-945-3585

Yonni's Italian Restaurant &
Bakery
19802 W Dixie Hwy.
North Miami Beach
305-932-1961

Yo Si Peking
Eden Roc Resort & Spa
4525 Collins Ave.
305-532-9060

Zigi's Yogurt
744 41st St.
305-531-6111

Orlando

Elaine's Cafe
3716 Howell Brand Rd.
407-679-9000

Kosher Korner*
4846 Palm Pkwy., Vista Center,
(across from Disney Village)
407-238-9968

The Lower East Side* (dinner)
Soho Coffee Shop (breakfast)
Catalina Inn Hotel
1-4 Exit 32 & John Young Pkwy.
(10 miles from Disney World)
407-648-4830

West Palm Beach

Steve Greensied Catering
407-697-9097

GEORGIA

Atlanta

Bian Catering
3130 Raymond Dr. NE
770-457-4578

Broadway Cafe*
2166 Briarcliff Rd.
404-329-0888
Vegetarian

Master Grill
3011 N. Druid Hills Rd.
404-325-3865
Middle Eastern

Toco Hills Kroger
2205 La Vista Rd.
404-633-8694

Wall Street Pizza
2470 Briarcliff Rd. NE
404-633-2111

The following Atlanta hotels have
kosher catering facilities: Atlanta
Marriott Perimeter, 246 Perimeter
Center Pkwy. NE, 770-698-6433;
Doubletree Hotel, 7 Concourse
Pkwy. NE, 770-395-3900; Holiday
Inn Crown Plaza Ravina, 4355
Ashford Dunwoody Rd. NE, 770-
395-7700; Sheraton Colony Square,
188 14th St. NE, 404-892-6000;
Swishôtel, 3391 Peachtree Rd. NE,
404-365-0065; Westin Peachtree
Plaza, 210 Peachtree St. NW, 404-
659-1400.

ILLINOIS

Chicago

Bugsy's
3353 Dempster
Skokie
874-679-4030

Danziger Kosher Caterers
Morton Grove
708-967-5511
Also caterer for 20 Chicago hotels

Delectables Unlimited Caterers
312-761-9613

Falafel King
4507 W. Oakton
Skokie
874-677-6020

Goldman-Segal Kosher Caterers
6814 N. Sacramento Ave.
Chicago 60645
312-338-4060

The Great Chicago Food &
Beverage Co.
Devon & Kedzie Sts.

Hungarian's Pizza & Pasta
4030 Oakton
Skokie
874-674-8008

Jerusalem Kosher Restaurant
3534 W. 63rd Ave.
312-776-6133

Ken's Diner
3353 Dempster, Skokie
847-679-4030

King Solomon
3445 Dempster, Skokie
847-677-0700

Kirshner Cuisine Caterers
2905 W. Fitch Ave.
312-465-6247

Kosher Gourmet
3552 W. Dempster
Skokie
312-679-8472
Chinese

Kosher Gourmet Caterers
Skokie
847-679-0597

Mi Tsu Yan Restaurant
3010 W. Devon Ave.
312-262-4630

Moishe's New York Kosher
2900 W. Devon Ave.

Polski Kosher Caterers
312-539-2288

Selig's Kosher Deli
209 Skokie Valley Rd.
Highland Park
312-831-5560

Slice of Life
4120 W. Dempster, Skokie
847-674-2021

Tel Aviv Kosher Pizza & Dairy
Restaurant
6349 N. California St.
312-764-3776

The following Chicago hotels have
their own kosher kitchens: Chicago
Hilton & Towers, 720 S. Michigan
Ave., 312-922-4400; Fairmont
Hotel, 200 N. Columbus Dr., 312-
565-8000; Hyatt Regency, 151 E.
Wacker Dr., 312-565-1234; North
Shore Hilton, 9599 Skokie Blvd.,
Skokie, 708-679-7000; Palmer
House Hilton, 171 E. Monroe St.,
312-726-7500.

LOUISIANA

New Orleans

Casablanca
3030 Severn Ave., Metaire
504-888-2209

Kosher Cajun Deli & Grocery*
3520 N. Hullen, Metaire
504-888-2010

MARYLAND

Baltimore

Chapp's of Pomona Restaurant
1700 Reisterstown Rd., Pikesville
410-653-3198

Danielle's Bluecrest*
401 Reisterstown Rd.
410-486-2100

Elite Catering
6505 Baythorne Rd.
410-655-5662

Ester Catering
6312 Benhurst Rd.

King David Bistro*
1777 Reisterstown Rd.

Knish Shop
508 Reisterstown Rd.
410-484-5850

Kosher Bite*
6309 Reisterstown Rd.
410-358-6349

Mama Leah's Gourmet Pizza
607-A Reisterstown Rd.

NYC Roasted
7105 Reisterstown Rd, Pikesville

O'Fishel Caterers
509 Reisterstown Rd.
410-764-3474

Premier Caterers
2624 Lord Baltimore Dr.
410-944-9000

Royal Restaurant*
7006A Reisterstown Rd.
410-727-5757

Shalom Caterers
4445 Old Court Rd.

Tov Pizza
6313 Reisterstown Rd.
410-358-5238

Weiss & Aviva Catering
6505 Baythorne Rd.

Kosher catering services are available at the Hyatt Regency on the Inner Harbor, 300 Light St., 410-528-1234, and at the Sheraton Inner Harbor Hotel, 410-962-8300.

MASSACHUSETTS

Boston

Cafe Shiraz*
1030 Commonwealth Ave.
617-566-8888
Persian & Middle Eastern cuisine

Catering by Andrew
404A Harvard St., Brookline
617-731-6585

Catering by Rubin
1500 Worcester Rd., Framingham
508-875-8096
345 Boylston St., Newton
617-965-7544

Catering by Simcha
33 Court Rd., Winthrop
617-846-6468

Green Manor Caterers
31 Tosca Dr., Stoughton
617-828-3018
345 Boylston St., Newton Centre
617-244-5344

Milk Street Cafe
50 Milk Street, Post Office Sq.
617-542-2433
Congress & Franklin Sts.
617-350-7275

Rami's Restaurant
324 Harvard St., Brookline
617-738-3577

Rubin's Restaurant
500 Harvard St., Brookline
617-566-8761

Shalom Hunan
92 Harvard St., Brookline
617-731-9760

Wald's Catering
634 Commonwealth Ave., Newton
617-965-1161

The following Boston hotels have kosher kitchens available for catered events: The Four Seasons Hotels, 200 Boylston St., 617-338-4400; Hyatt Regency Cambridge, 575 Memorial Dr., 617-492-1234; Park Plaza Hotel, 64 Arlington St., 617-426-2000; Westin Hotel, 10 Huntington Ave., 617-262-9600.

MICHIGAN

Detroit

New York Pizza World
15280 Lincoln (10.5 Mile Rd.),
Oak Park
810-968-2102

Unique Kosher Carryout
25270 Greenfield Rd., Oak Park
810-967-1161

MINNESOTA

Minneapolis

Fishman's Kosher
4000 Minnetonka Blvd.
612-926-5611

Old City Cafe
1571 Grand Ave.
612-699-5347
Vegetarian

MISSOURI

St. Louis

Adventures Unlimited Catering
314-426-4477

Lazy Susan Catering
314-291-6050

No Bull Cafe
10477 Old Olive St. Rd.
314-991-9533
Vegetarian

Reservations Catering
314-205-2900

Simon Kohn Enterprises*
10424 Old Olive St. Rd.
314-569-0727

Sol's*
8627 Olive St. Rd.
314-993-9977

The following St. Louis hotels are available for kosher catering: Adam Mark Hotel, 4th & Chestnut, 314-241-7400; Frontenac Hilton, 1335 S. Lindbergh, Frontenac, 314-993-1100; Hyatt Regency, 1 St. Louis St., Union Station, 314-231-1234; Marriott Airport, 1-70 Lambert International Airport, 314-423-9700; Ritz Carleton, 100 Carondelet Plaza, Clayton, 314-863-6300.

NEVADA

Las Vegas

Casba
855 E. Twain Ave.
702-791-3344

Jerusalem
1305 Vegas Valley Dr.
702-696-1644

Rafi's Place
6135 W. Sahara Ave.
702-253-0033

NEW JERSEY

Atlantic County

Jerusalem Kosher Restaurant
6410 Ventnor Ave., Ventnor
(Atlantic City area)
609-822-2266

Bergen County

Fliegels
456 Cedar Ln., Teaneck
201-692-8060

Foremost Caterers
58 Jefferson Ave., Westwood
201-664-2465

Hunan Teaneck
515 Cedar Ln., Teaneck
201-692-0099

JC Pizza
14-20 Plaza Rd., Fair Lawn
201-703-0801

JC Pizza at Jerusalem V
24 W. Palisade Ave., Englewood
201-569-5546

Jerusalem Pizza
496 Cedar Ln., Teaneck
201-836-2120

Kosher Memories Caterers
Teaneck
201-833-0501

The Kosher Nosh
894 Prospect St., Glen Rock
201-445-1186

Ma'bat Steak House
540 Cedar Ln., Teaneck
201-836-4115

Main Event Caterers
439 Cedar Lane, Teaneck
201-836-1600

Noah's Ark*
493 Cedar Ln., Teaneck
201-692-1200

Plaza Pizza & Restaurant
1431 Queen Anne Rd., Teaneck
201-837-9500

Shelly's
482 Cedar Ln., Teaneck
201-692-0001

Middlesex County

Feltus/Aunt Zelda & Co. Caterers
271 U.S. 1 S., Edison
908-985-6363

Monmouth County

Chang Mao Sakura Chinese &
Japanese Restaurant
214 Roosevelt Ave., Oakhurst
(Deal)
908-517-8889†

Morris County

Beck's Best Deli
76 N. Beverwyck Rd., Lake
Hiawatha
201-263-9515††

---

†As of June 1, 1997, the area code
for this number will be 732.
††As of June 1, 1997, the area code
for this number will be 973.

Passaic County

China Pagoda
227 Main Ave., Passaic
201-777-4900††

Jerusalem Pizza & Falafel 2
224 Brook Ave., Passaic
201-778-0960††

Union County

The Newark Airport Hilton, 1170
Spring St., Elizabeth, 908-351-
3900, has separate kosher catering
facilities.

NEW YORK

Bronx

Mr. Bagel*
5672 Broadway
718-549-0408

The Corner Cafe & Bakery
3552 Johnson Ave.
718-601-2861

Riverdelight Restaurant
3534 Johnson Ave.
718-543-4270

The Main Event*
3708 Riverdale Ave.
718-601-3013, 718-601-MAIN (for
catering)

Szechuan Garden
3717 Riverdale Ave.
718-884-4242

---

††As of June 1, 1997, the area code
for this number will be 973.

Brooklyn

A Catered Mazel Affair Dairy
Restaurant
4807 New Utrecht Ave.
718-854-3753

Adelman's Deli
1906 King's Highway
718-336-4915

Alex Klein Caterers
718-339-4466

Brighton Beach Dairy
Restaurant/Brand's Gourmet Food
410 Brighton Beach Ave.
718-646-7421

Cachet Restaurant
815 Kings Highway
718-336-8600

Cafe Kapulsky
1217 Ave. J
718-338-3646

Carmel Glatt Kosher Restaurant
523 Kings Highway
718-339-0172

Catering by Ezra
60 Brighton 11th St.
718-336-1101

Chadash Pizza
1919 Avenue M
718-253-4793

Chap-A-Nosh
1424 Elm Ave.
718-627-0072

China Glatt*
4413 13th Ave.
718-438-2576

Coney Island Deli*
1359 Coney Island Ave.
718-253-1002

D. Zion Burger Restaurant
4102 18th Ave.
718-871-9467

Dagan Pizza
1560 Ralph Ave.
718-209-0636

Dairyland Restaurant
3342 Nostrand Ave.
718-615-0222

Edna's Restaurant & Deli*
125 Church Ave.
718-438-8207

Essex on Coney Restaurant*
1359 Coney Island Ave.
718-253-1002

Fifth Avenue Caterers
718-868-1717

Flatbush Catering & Takeout
1383 Coney Island Ave.
718-252-8888

Fountain Blue French & Moroccan
Cuisine*
712 Ave. U
718-339-5805

Fuji Hana Japanese Restaurant
512 Ave. U
718-336-3888

Gracious Host Caterers
1211 Ave. J
718-338-7660

H&J Quality Caterers & Appetizers
1504 Albany Ave.
718-434-0700

Ice Cream Center
4511 13th Ave.
718-438-0018

Jerusalem Kosher Pizza
1312 Ave. J
718-338-8156

Jerusalem Steak House
533 Kings Hwy.
718-336-5115
Moroccan & Mediterranean

Jerusalem II Gardens Cafe
817 Kings Hwy.
718-998-0210

Kennereth Glatt Kosher Caterers
1920 Ave. U
718-743-2473

King Deli
924 Kings Hwy.
718-336-7555

King's Bamboo Garden
904 Kings Hwy.
718-375-8501
Vegetarian Chinese

Kingsbay Caterers
3692 Nostrand Ave.
718-891-7178

Kingsway Caterers
2902 Kings Hwy.
718-338-5000

Knish King
2916 Ave. M
718-377-6218

Kosher Castle
5006 13th Ave.
718-436-7474

Kosher Court
52 Court St.
718-237-0226

Kosher Delight
4600 13th Ave.
718-435-8500
1223 Ave. J
718-377-6873

Kosher Hut
709 Kings Hwy.
718-376-8999

Landau's Glatt Kosher Deli
65 Lee Ave.
718-782-3700

L&E Kosher Caterers
1710 Ave. M
718-375-7919

Le Chateau/Pruzansky Family
Caterers
431 Ave. P
718-339-0200

Locker Caterers
718-258-7088

Mama's Restaurant
906 Kings Highway
718-382-7200

Mazel Restaurant and Caterers
4807 New Utrecht Ave.
718-854-3753

McDaniel's Pizza
549 Kings Hwy.
718-627-9668

Meisner's Glatt Kosher
1312 55th St.
718-436-5529

Melrose Take Home Foods &
Catering
1500 Sheepshead Bay Rd.
718-891-2442
268 Brighton Beach Rd.
718-646-6460

Natanya Chinese Restaurant
1204 Ave. J
718-258-5160

Negev Food Caterers
1211 Ave. J
718-258-8440

Nosheria
4813 13th Ave.
718-436-0400

Oneg Take Out & Caterers
4911 12th Ave.
718-438-3388

Oriental
2684 Nostrand Ave.
718-338-0809
Chinese, Korean, Japanese &
Vietnamese cuisines

Ossie's Table
1314 50th St.
718-435-0635

Risshon Pizza
5114 13th Ave.
718-438-9226

Ruthy's Catering
547 Kings Hwy.
718-339-1201

Say Cheese
1304 Ave. M
718-998-8778

Say Chicken
1681 E 16th St.
718-627-1615

Shalom Hunan
1619 Ave. M
718-382-6000

Shang Chai Kosher Restaurant
2189 Flatbush Ave.
718-377-6100

Sixteenth Avenue Bagel & Pizza
4303 16th Ave.
718-871-5254

Sushi Kosher*
1626 Coney Island Ave.
718-338-6363

Tehila Mon Jardin
811 Kings Hwy.
718-339-9733

Tropper Ltd. Caterers
718-258-9006

Weiss Kosher Dairy Restaurant*
1146 Coney Island Ave.
718-421-0184

Yunkee
1424 Elm Ave.
718-627-0072
Chinese-American

Manhattan

Abigael's
9 E. 37th St.
212-725-0130

Alexi on 56*
25 West 56th St.
212-767-1234

All American Health & Cafe Bar*
24 E. 42nd St.
212-370-4525

American Cafe, Health Bar &
Pizza*
160 Broadway
212-732-1426

Ben's Kosher Delicatessen
209 W. 38th St.
212-398-2367

Bissaleh Classic Dairy Restaurant
1435 Second Ave.
212-717-2333
Middle Eastern

Broadway's Jerusalem 2 Pizza
1375 Broadway
212-398-1475

Cafe 18
8 E. 18th St.
212-620-4182

Cafe Classico*
25 W. 57th St.
212-355-5411

Cafe Masada*
1239 First Ave.
212-988-0950

Cafe 1-2-3
2 Park Ave.
212-685-7117

Cafe Roma Pizzeria
459 Park Ave. S.
212-683-3044

Cafe Yarden
285 Columbus Ave.
212-721-5333

China Shalom II*
686 Columbus Ave.
212-662-9676

Colbeh Restaurant
43 W. 39th St.
212-354-8181

Deli Glatt Sandwich Shop
150 Fulton St.
212-349-3622

Deli Kasbah BBQ & Grill
251 W. 85th St.
212-496-1500
2553 Amsterdam Ave.
212-568-4600

Dougie's BBQ & Grill
222 W. 72nd St.
212-724-2222

Empire Kosher Chicken Restaurant
2014 Broadway
212-721-2508

Essen West Take Out*
226 W. 72nd St.
212-362-1234

Esti Hana Oriental Noodle Shop &
Sushi Bar
221 W. 79th St.
215-501-0393

Fellini
12 E. 49th St.
212-832-2500

Fine & Schapiro
Kosher Restaurant and
Delicatessen
138 W. 78th St.
212-877-2721

Galil Restaurant
1252 Lexington Ave.
212-439-9886
Israeli & Moroccan

G&M Kosher Caterers
41 Essex St.
212-254-5370
Hungarian

Glatt Dynasty Chinese Restaurant*
1049 2nd Ave.
212-888-9119

Grand American Health Bar
49 Ann St.
212-587-8101

Grand Deli Chinese-American*
399 Grand St.
212-477-5200

Great American Health and
Espresso Bar
35 W. 57th St.
212-355-5177

Haikara Japanese Grill
1016 2nd Ave.
212-355-7000

Har Zion Tasty Restaurant
325 Fifth Ave.
212-213-1110

IDT Mega Lite Cafe
19 W. 45th St.
The country's only kosher cyber-
cafe

Jasmine Persian Restaurant*
11 E. 30th St.
212-251-8884

Joseph's*
50 W. 72nd St.
212-595-5004 restaurant,
212-875-0689 catering

Ken & David Kosher Delicatessen*
249 E. 45th St.
212-986-4704

Kosher Dairy Luncheonette
23 W. 19th St.
212-645-9315

Kosher Delight
1156 Ave. of Americas
212-869-6699
1359 Broadway
212-563-3366

Kosher Heaven
55 Ann St.
212-587-1185

Kosher Tea Room
193 2nd Ave.
212-677-2947

La Fontana
309 E. 83rd St.
212-734-6343

L'Chaim Caterers & Take Out Food
Store
4464 Broadway
212-304-4852

Le Marais Bistro & Steakhouse
150 W. 46th St.
212-869-0900

Levana Restaurant*
141 W. 69th St.
212-877-8457

Lou G Siegel Catering
240 W. 14th St.
212-921-4433

Madras Mahal
104 Lexington Ave.
212-684-4010
Indian vegetarian

Mendy's Steak House, Delicatessen
& Bar
61 E. 34th St.
212-576-1010

Mendy's West Restaurant & Sports
Club
208 W. 70th St.
212-877-6787

Mom's Bagels & Dairy*
15 W. 45th St.
212-764-1566

Mr. Broadway Kosher Deli/Me Tsu
Yan
1372 Broadway
212-921-2152
Kosher Chinese food

My Favorite Dessert Company
Restaurant & Cafe
120 W. 45th St.
212-997-5130

Papilsky Caterers
210 W. 91st St.
212-724-3761

Pizza Plus
2500 Amsterdam Ave.
212-927-5858

Pongal
110 Lexington Ave.
212-696-9458
Indian vegetarian

Provi, Provi*
228 W. 72nd St.
212-875-9020

Ratner's Kosher Restaurant
138 Delancey St.
212-677-5588

Royale Kosher Bake Shop & Cafe
237 W. 72nd St.
212-874-5642

Second Avenue Kosher Deli*
156 Second Ave.
212-677-0606

Shalom Chai Pizza
359 Grand St.
212-598-1178

Shalom Kosher Pizza
100 Ave. of Americas
212-730-0008

Shira Pizza
63 Reade St.
212-267-5075

Siegel's Kosher Deli & Restaurant
1435 2nd Ave.
212-288-2094
1646 2nd Ave.
212-288-3632

Table Classics Kosher Caterers
210 W. 101st St.
212-316-2430

Tevere "84" Italian Restaurant
155 E. 84th St.
212-744-0210

Time Out Pizza
2549 Amsterdam Ave.
212-923-1180

Va Bene Kosher Ristorante Italiano
1589 2nd Ave.
212-517-4448

Vegetable Garden Dairy Restaurant
& Caterer
15 E. 40th St.
212-545-7444

Vegetarian Heaven Chinese
Restaurant
304 W. 58th St.
212-956-4678

Vege Vege II
544 3rd Ave.
212-679-4710

Village Crown Italian Dairy
Cuisine*
94 3rd Ave.
212-777-8816

Village Crown Restaurant &
Garden Cafe
96 3rd Ave.
212-674-2061
Moroccan, Middle Eastern, vegetarian

What's Cooking Restaurant*
18 E. 41st St.
212-725-6096

Yummi Restaurant BBQ & Grill
63 Reade St.
212-587-8204

Most major New York City hotels can
make arrangements for kosher catering.

Queens

Bamboo Garden
41-28 Main St., Flushing
718-463-9240
Vegetarian Chinese

Ben's Bayside Restaurant*
211-37 26th Ave., Bayside
718-229-2367

Ben's Best Kosher Deli &
Restaurant*
96-40 Queens Blvd., Rego Park
718-897-1700

Berso Take Home Foods and
Catering
64–20 108th St.
Forest Hills
718-275-9793

Beth Torah Glatt Kosher Caterers
106-06 Queens Blvd., Forest Hills
718-261-4775

Bombay Kitchen (Indian)*
113-25 Queens Blvd., Forest Hills
718-263-4733

Burger Nosh*
69-48 Main St., Kew Gardens Hills

Catering by Celebration
Mauzone's
67-11 73rd Ave.,
Flushing
718-591-0235

Cho-Sen Garden*
64-43 108th St., Forest Hills
718-275-1300

Club Rafael Restaurant*
116-29 Queens Blvd., Forest Hills
718-260-3308

David's Kosher Deli/Kosher Club*
58-80 Maurice Ave., Maspeth
718-326-0568

Deli Express*
67-21 Main St.,
Kew Gardens Hills
718-793-3061

Deli Master
184-02 Horace Harding Expwy.,
Fresh Meadows
718-353-3030

Empire Roasters Restaurant
180-30 Union Tpke.
Fresh Meadows
718-591-4220
100-19 Queens Blvd., Forest Hills
718-997-7135

Fifth Avenue Caterers
23-55 Healey Ave., Far Rockaway
718-868-1717

Full Moon Garden*
167-01 Union Tpke.,
Fresh Meadows
718-380-2828
Chinese/Japanese

Glatt Wok Express Take-Out
190-11 Union Tpke.,
Fresh Meadows
718-740-1675

Glatt Wok Palace Restaurant
190-13 Union Tpke.,
Fresh Meadows
718-740-1362

Habait
98-102 Queens Blvd., Forest Hills
718-897-4829
Yemenite cuisine

Hapina, Hapina
69-54 Main St., Kew Gardens Hills
718-544-6262

Hapisgah Steakhouse
147-25 Union Turnpike,
Kew Gardens Hills
718-380-4449

Jerusalem Cafe*
72-02 Main St., Kew Gardens Hills
718-520-8940

King Solomon Kosher Pizza
75-43 Main St.
Kew Gardens Hills
718-793-0710

Kingsway Caterers
193-10 Peck Ave.,
Fresh Meadows
718-357-4585

Kinneret Deli & Catering
96-35 Queens Blvd., Rego Park
718-897-6100

Kosher Corner Dairy Restaurant*
73-31 Main St., Kew Gardens Hills
718-263-1177

Kosher Haven Caterers
65-30 Kissena Blvd., Flushing
718-261-0149

Kosher King Deli
72-30 Main St., Kew Gardens Hills
718-793-5464

Lassova Restaurant
64-29 108th St., Forest Hills
718-897-1450
Middle Eastern cuisine

Lederman Caterers
203-05 32nd Ave., Bayside
718-352-6564

Mabat Steak House
68-36 Main St., Kew Gardens Hills
718-793-2926

Maven Take Out*
188-09 Union Tpke.,
Jamaica Estates
718-479-5504

Mauzone Home Kosher Products*
61-36 Springfield Blvd.
Bayside
718-255-1188
69-60 Main St.
Kew Gardens Hills
718-261-7723

Mazurs Market Place/Restaurant
254-51 Horace Harding Blvd.,
Little Neck
718-428-5000

Meal Mart on Main Street Caterers
72-10 Main St., Kew Gardens Hills
718-261-3300

Mirage Restaurant
181-34 Union Tpke.
Fresh Meadows
718-591-0136

Moishe's Kosher Pizza & Dairy
Restaurant
181-30 Union Tpke.
Fresh Meadows
718-969-1928

Naomi's Kosher Pizza
68-28 Main St.
Kew Garden Hills
718-520-8754

Or Yehuda Kosher Restaurant
138-44 86th St., Jamaica
718-291-3406

Pastrami King Kosher Restaurant
& Deli*
124-24 Queens Blvd., Kew Gardens
718-263-1717

Prestige Caterers
210-10 Union Tpke., Flushing
718-464-8400

Salut Kosher Restaurant
63-42 108th St., Forest Hills
718-275-6860

Sandy's Surf Delicatessen*
101-05 Queens Blvd., Forest Hills
718-459-7875

Shimon's Pizza & Falafel
71-24 Main St., Kew Gardens Hills
718-793-1491

Shirley's Place Kosher Deli &
Restaurant
78-16 Linden Blvd., Howard Beach
718-296-3064

Stargate*
73-27 Main St., Kew Gardens Hills
718-793-1199

Tajikistan
102-03A Queens Blvd., Forest Hills
718-830-0744
Afghan

The Wok
100–21 Queens Blvd.
Forest Hills
718-896-0310

Toy Caterers
97-22 63rd Rd., Rego Park
718-896-7788

Staten Island

Dairy Palace
2210 Victory Blvd.
718-761-5200

Long Island

Bagel Boss Cafe*
432 S. Oyster Bay Rd., Hicksville
516-935-9079, 888-BOSSTIME for
catering
10 Jericho Tpke., Jericho
516-334-0300
405 Merrick Rd., Oceanside
516-766-1581
2101 Merrick Rd., Merrick
516-379-2836

Ben's Kosher Catering
516-427-2367

Ben's Kosher Delicatessen*
Wheatley Plaza, Greenvale
516-621-3340
95 Old Country Rd., Carle Place
516-742-3354
135 Alexander Ave.
Lake Grove
516-979-8770
437 N. Broadway, Jericho
516-939-2367
933 Atlantic Ave., Baldwin
516-868-2072

Bon Appetit Caterers
381 Willis Ave., Rosyln Heights
516-621-1412
All diet foods

Carltun Kosher Caterers
108 Old Mill Rd., Great Neck
516-829-6666

The Cedars Club*
564 Central Ave., Cedarhurst
516-374-1714

Cho-Sen Island*
367 Central Ave., Lawrence
516-374-1199

Colbeh Restaurant
75 North Plaza, Great Neck
516-466-8181

Hunan
507 Middle Neck Rd., Great Neck
516-482-7912

Jem Prestige Caterers
200 Southwoods Rd., Woodbury
516-364-2000

Kay Caterers
111 Irving Pl., Woodmere
516-374-5657

King David Delicatessen &
Caterers
550 Central Ave., Cedarhurst
516-569-2920

Kings Point Grill
9 Cuttermill Rd.
Great Neck
516-482-7475
Israeli cuisine

Kosher World Caterers
177 Hempstead Ave.
West Hempstead
516-489-2700

Model K Caterers
3445 Lawson Blvd., Oceanside
516-766-2318

Mr. Omelette Caterers
3445 Lawson Blvd., Oceanside
516-766-1884, 800-625-6474

President Caterers
1400 Prospect Ave.,
East Meadow
516-483-4991
2860 Brower Ave., Oceanside
516-536-6387

Sapienza Restaurant
1376 Hempstead Tpke., Elmont
516-352-5232

Scharf Caterers
597A Willow Rd., Cedarhurst
516-295-5959

Shop Glatt*
172 E. Park Ave.,
Long Beach
516-897-8657

Silver Caterers of the Five Towns
Broadway & Locust Ave.,
Cedarhurst
516-791-2046
410 Hungry Harbor Rd., North
Woodmere
800-7-SILVER

Simon's Restaurant*
1066 Broadway, Woodmere
516-374-2591

Simply Delicious Gourmet
Appetizing and Caterers
429 Merrick Rd., Oceanside
516-594-4400

Talia's Cafe Italian Restaurant
582 Central Ave.,
Cedarhurst
516-569-2162

Traditions Restaurant*
302 Central Ave.,
Lawrence
516-295-3630

Woodbury Glatt Kosher Catering
428 S. Oyster Bay Rd., Hicksville
516-681-7766

Woodro Kosher Restaurant*
1342 Peninsula Blvd., Hewlitt
516-791-4033

Zomick's Kafe
444 Central Ave., Cedarhurst
516-569-5520

The Best Western Hotel, 80 Clinton
St., Hempstead, 516-486-4100, has a
kosher kitchen for catered events.

Rockland County

Al Di La Kosher Dairy Restaurant
455 Rte. 306, Wesley Hills Plaza,
Monsey
914-354-2672

Bagels 'n More
106 B Route 59, Monsey

Glatt Wok
106 C Rte. 59
Monsey
914-352-1994

Jerusalem Pizza
190 Rte. 59, Monsey

Pulkie's Glatt Kosher Restaurant
Wesley Hills Plaza, Rte. 306,
Monsey
914-362-7855

Ram Caterers
Monsey
914-352-0733

Wilton Caterers
Spring Valley
914-352-4800

Westchester County

Adam's Rib Grill Room & Deli*
1305 North Ave., New Rochelle
914-636-4381

Ardsley Kosher Restaurant
Ardsley Mall, 935 Saw Mill River
Rd., Ardsley
914-693-2232

Betay-ah-Von
1126 Wilmot Rd., Scarsdale
914-472-3597

Classic Caterers
914-638-0702

Epstein's Kosher Restaurant*
387 Central Ave, Hartsdale
914-428-5320
2369 Central Park Ave., Yonkers
914-793-3131

Prime Time Pasta
1319 North Ave., New Rochelle
914-654-1646

Waterfall Caterers
914-578-1690

The Rye Town Hilton, 699 Westchester
Ave., Rye Brook, 914-939-6300, and the
Renaissance Hotel, White Plains, 914-
694-5400, have kosher catering facilities.

OHIO

Cincinnati

Tel Aviv Cafe
7384 Reading Rd.
513-631-8808

Cleveland

Empire Kosher Chicken Restaurant
2234 Warrensville Center Rd.,
University Heights
216-691-0006

Kinneret Kosher Pizza
1869 S. Taylor Rd.,
Cleveland Heights
216-321-1404

Columbus

The Kosher Buckeye
2944 E. Broad St.
614-235-8070

Mezzanine Kosher Restaurant
700 N. High St.
614-228-4857

Sammy's New York Bagels & Deli
Corner Broad St. & James Rd.

OREGON

Portland

Allen Levine
Garbanzos Catering
503-227-4196

Noah's Bagels
3541 SE Hawthorn Blvd.
503-731-8855

PENNSYLVANIA

Lehigh & Northampton Counties

Abe's Place Deli Restaurant
1741 Allen St., Allentown
610-435-1735

Catering by Ann
610-664-5327

Philadelphia

Cherry Street Chinese Vegetarian
1010 Cherry St.
215-923-3663

Dragon Inn Chinese Restaurant
7628 Castor Ave.
215-742-2575

Essene Cafe
719 S. Fourth St.
215-922-1146
Organic vegetarian

Kosher Creations Catering
215-342-3961

Maccabean
128 S. 11th St.
215-922-5922

Rajbhog Restaurant
& Sweets
738 Adams Ave.
215-853-1937
Indian vegetarian

Singapore Chinese Vegetarian
Restaurant
1029 Race St.
215-922-3288

Tiberias Cafeteria
8010 Castor Ave.
215-725-7444

Traditions Restaurant
9550 Bustleton Ave.
215-677-2221

The Water Wheel
1529 Sansom St.
215-563-9601

Zev's Catering
215-477-0864

The Wyndom Franklin Plaza, 17th
& Race Sts., 215-448-2000, has
kosher catering facilities.

Pittsburgh

King David Chinese Restaurant
2020 Murray Ave.
412-422-3370

Yacov's Vegetarian Restaurant
2109 Murray Ave.
412-421-7208

TENNESSEE

Memphis

Jon's Place
764 Mt. Moriah
901-374-0600

M. I. Gottlieb's
5062 Park Avenue, East Gate
Shopping Center
901-763-3663

TEXAS

Dallas

Deco's by Arthur
Preston-Forest Shopping
Center NW
214-788-2808

Kosher Link
7517 Campbell Rd.
214-248-3773

Houston

Drumsticks
10200 S. Main
713-664-8885

Nosher, Inc.
2 Braeswood Sq.
713-721-3883

Simon's Gourmet Kosher Foods
5411 S. Braeswood
713-729-5333

Wonderful Vegetarian Restaurant
7549 Westheimer
713-977-3137
Chinese

WASHINGTON

Seattle

Bamboo Gardens Vegetarian
Cuisine
364 Roy St.
206-282-6616

Bitay Avone
Pike Place Market
206-448-5597

Kosher Delight
1509 First Ave. & Pike St.
206-682-8140

Park Deli*
5011 S. Dawson St.
206-722-6674

CANADA

Calgary, Alberta

Karen's Cafe*
Jewish Cultural Center,
1607-90th Ave.
403-225-5311

Montreal, Quebec

Casa Linga
5095 Queen Mary Rd.
514-737-2272

El Morrocco II
3450 Drummond
514-844-6888

Ernie & Ellie's Place
6900 DeCarie Blvd.
514-344-4444

Foxy's Kosher Pizza
5987 Victoria Ave.
514-739-8777

Galil Glatt Kosher
5887 Victoria Ave.
514-733-7770
Israeli cuisine

Kotel
3429 Peel
514-987-9875
Middle Eastern cuisine

Mitchell's Restaurant
5500 Westbury
514-737-8704

Pizza Pita
5710 Victoria
514-731-7482

Restaurant Passeport
5071 Queen Mary Rd.

Tel Aviv Restaurant
4961B Queen Mary Rd.
514-345-9243

Yossi's Dizengoff Cafe
3460 Stanley St.
514-845-9171
Israeli cuisine

Toronto, Ontario

Bagels Galore
First Canadian Pl. Tower
416-363-4233

Cafe Sheli
Clark Ave., Thornhill

Chicken Nest
3038 Bathurst St.
416-787-6378

Dairy Treats
3522 Bathurst St.
416-787-0309

Hakerem
1045 Steeles Ave. W.
416-736-7227

King David's Pizza
3020 Bathurst St.
416-781-1326

Kosher Delights 24 Hour Cafe
7241 Bathurst St., Thornhill
905-731-3831

Marky's Delicatessen
280 Wilson Ave.
416-638-1001
7330 Yonge St.
905-731-4800

Milk 'N Honey
3457 Bathurst St.
416-789-7651

My Zaidy's Bagel & Pizza
3426 Bathurst St.
416-789-0785

Perl's Deli
3013 Bathurst St.
416-787-4234

Tov Li Pizza
5972 Bathurst St.
416-650-9800

Vancouver, British Columbia

Sabra 2
950 W. 41st Ave.
604-257-5111

Tel Aviv
49th & Oak Sts.
604-736-5888

Winnipeg, Manitoba

Desserts Plus*
1595 Main St.
204-339-1957

Downstairs Deli
Main & McAdam
204-338-4991

MEXICO

Acapulco

El Isleño Restaurant, in Hyatt
Regency Acapulco Hotel
800 233 1234

Mexico City

Pizzas Koshertel
Various locations

BAKERIES, BUTCHERS, AND MARKETS

Note: A number of supermarket chains and discount shopping clubs carry selections of kosher products, including poultry and baked goods. These include Acme, America's Choice, Costco, C-Town, Finast, Food Emporium, Foodtown, Grand Union, King Kullen, Pathmark, Price Club, ShopRite, Super Fresh, and Waldbaum's.

ARIZONA

Phoenix

Karsh's Bakery
5539 N. 7th St.
602-264-4874

Segal's Kosher Foods
4818 N. 7th St.
602-285-1515

S n Z Kosher
5132 Camelback Rd., Glendale
602-939-7309

CALIFORNIA

Long Beach

Los Alamitos Kosher Meat and
Poultry
11196 Los Alamitos Blvd.,
Los Alamitos
310-594-4609

Los Angeles

Back East Bialy Bakery
8562 W. Pico Blvd.,
310-276-1531

Beverly Hills Patisserie
9100 W. Pico Blvd.
310-275-6873

BH International Bakery
7304¼ Santa Monica Blvd.
213-874-7456

Carmel Kosher Meats
8914 W. Pico Blvd.
310-278-6347

City Glatt
7667 Beverly Blvd.
213-933-4040

Doheny Kosher Meats
9213 W. Pico Blvd.
310-276-7232

Dove's Bakery
8924 W. Pico Blvd.
310-276-6150

Eilat Bakery
513 N. Fairfax Blvd.
213-653-5553
9233 W. Pico Blvd.
310-205-8700

Elat Market
8730 W. Pico Blvd.
310-659-7070

Fairfax Fish
515 N. Fairfax Ave.
213-658-8060

Famous Bakery
350 N. Fairfax Ave.
213-933-5000

Kosher Klub Butcher & Market
4817 W. Pico Blvd.
213-933-8283

Kotlar's Pico Market
8622 W. Pico Blvd.
310-652-5355

La Brea Kosher Market
410 N. La Brea Ave.
213-931-1221

Le Palais Bakery
8670 W. Pico Blvd.
310-659-4809

Little Jerusalem Market
8917 W. Pico Blvd.
310-858-8361

New York Kosher Market
16733 Ventura Blvd., Encino
818-788-0007

Pico Glatt Kosher Mart
9427 W. Pico Blvd.
310-785-0904

Rami Meat Market
505 N. Fairfax Ave.
213-651-4293

Renaissance Bakery
22872 Ventura Blvd.
818-222-0110

Royal Fish
8973 W. Pico Blvd.
310-859-0632

Roz Kosher Meats & Market
12422-24 Burbank Blvd.
818-760-7694

Sam's Kosher Bakery
12450 Burbank Blvd.
818-769-8352

Schwartz's Bakery
441 N. Fairfax Blvd.
213-653-1683
8616 W. Pico Blvd.
310-854-0592

Star Meats
12136 Santa Monica Blvd.
310-447-1612

Valley Glatt Market
12836½ Victory Blvd.,
North Hollywood
818-506-5542

Valley Glatt Meats
12450 Burbank Blvd.,
North Hollywood
818-766-4530

Ventura Market
18357 Ventura Blvd.
213-873-1240

Western Kosher Market
444 N. Fairfax Ave.
213-655-8870

Palo Alto

Molly Stones Market
164 S. California Ave.
415-323-8361

Sacramento

Bob's Butcher Block Grocery &
Deli
6436 Fair Oaks Blvd., Carmichael
Oaks Shopping Center
916-482-6884

San Francisco

Israel Kosher Meat & Poultry
Market & Deli
5621 Geary Blvd.
415-752-3064

Tel Aviv Kosher Meat Market
1301 Noriega St.
415-661-7588

Wedemeyer's Bakery
314 Harbor Way
415-873-1000

San Jose

Willow Glen Kosher Market
1185 Lincoln Ave.
408-297-6604

COLORADO

Denver

B & J's Utica Grocery
4500 West Colfax Ave.
303-534-2253

Eastside Kosher Grocery
5475 Leetsdale Dr.
303-322-9862

New York Bagel Boys
6449 E. Hampden Ave.
303-759-2212

CONNECTICUT

Bridgeport

Brooklawn Bakery
1718 Capitol Ave.
203-384-0504

Whims and Wishes
1445 Capitol Ave.
203-368-2412

Hartford

Crown Market Deli & Bakery
2471 Albany Ave., West Hartford
860-236-1965

New Haven

Fox's Deli & Bakery
140 Whalley Ave.
203-397-0839

Westville Kosher Bakery
Whalley Ave.
203-387-2214

Westville Kosher Meat Market
Whalley Ave.
203-389-1166

Stamford

Cerebone's Bakery
605 Newfield Ave.
203-348-9029

Delicate-Essen Meat, Poultry &
Grocery
111 High Ridge Rd.
203-316-5570

Waterbury

Ami's Hot Bagels
111 Tomaston Ave.
203-594-9020

FLORIDA

Boca Raton

Boca Kosher Meats
9070 Kimberly Blvd.
407-488-9808

Oriole Kosher Meats
7351 W. Atlantic Ave.
407-427-8722

Star of David Meats
1806 W. Hillsboro Blvd.,
Deerfield Beach
407-427-6400

Fort Myers

Bubee's Kosher Foods
1939 Park Meadows Dr.
941-278-5674

Miami Beach

Abraham's Kosher Bakery
7423 Collins Ave.
305-861-0191

Abraham's Kosher Baker II
757 NE 167th St., North Miami
Beach
305-652-3343

Glatt Town Grocery & Butcher
Shop
1123 NE 163rd St., North Miami
Beach
305-944-7726

Kastner's Pastry Shop
7440 Collins Ave.
305-865-8217

Kosher Gourmet Gallery
456 41st St., North Miami Beach
305-535-7444

Kosher World
514 41st St.
305-532-2210

Pastry Lane Bakery
1688 NE 164th St., North Miami Beach
305-944-5934

Pastry Lane Bakery II
4022 Royal Palm Ave.
305-674-9523

Orlando

Kosher Korner
4846 Palm Pkwy., Vista Center
(across from Disney World)
407-238-9968

West Palm Beach

Century Kosher Market
4869 Okeechobee Blvd.
407-686-2066

Chiffon Kosher Bakery
1253 Old Okeechobee Rd.
407-833-7404

GEORGIA

Atlanta

Bernie the Baker
3015 N. Druid Hills Rd. NE
404-633-1986

Kg's Bakery & Stuff
2088 Briarcliff Rd.
404-321-1166

Kroger Kosher Fish, Meat & Deli
2205 Lavista Rd. NE
404-633-8694

Quality Kosher Emporium
2153 Briarcliff Rd. NE
404-636-1114
5942 Roswell Rd.,
Hammond Square
800-305-6328, 404-705-8643

ILLINOIS

Chicago

Chaim's Kosher Bakery, Deli, & Supermarket
4956 W. Dempster, Skokie

Gitel's Bakery
2745 W. Devon Ave.

Hungarian Kosher Foods
4020 Oakton, Skokie
847-674-8008
Butcher, deli, bakery, grocery

King David's Kosher Bakery
1731 Howard, Evanston
312-475-0270

Kosher Kary Deli & Grocery Store
2828 W Devon Ave., Skokie

Lippman Kosher Meat Market
6702 N. Crawford Ave.,
Lincolnwood
312-674-6105

Main Street Kosher Meat & Poultry
4002 Main Street, Skokie
847-677-5188

North Shore Kosher Bakery
2919 W. Touhy

Roumanian Kosher Sausage Company
7200 North Clark
312-761-4141

Shaevitz Kosher Meat &
Delicatessen
712 Central Ave., Highland Park
312-432-8334

Shalom Bakery
1165 Arlington Heights Rd.,
Buffalo Grove

Sinai Kosher Sausage Company
100 W. Pershing Rd.

Slovin & Soloman Kosher Meat
4004 Main, Skokie
847-673-3737

Tel Aviv Bakery
2944 W. Devon Ave.
312-764-8877

Tel Aviv Kosher Shopping Plaza
4956 Dempster, Skokie
847-675-1005

LOUISIANA

New Orleans

Dorignac's Food Center
710 Veteran's Memorial Blvd.,
Metaire
504-834-8216

MAINE

Portland

Penny Wise Supermarket
182 Ocean Ave.
207-772-8808

MARYLAND

Baltimore

Goldman's Kosher Bakery &
Pastry Shop
6848 Reisterstown Rd.
410-358-9625

Mirakle Market
6836 Reisterstown Rd.
410-358-3443

Pariser's Bakery
6711 Reisterstown Rd.
410-764-1700

Schmell & Azman Bakery
7006 Reisterstown Rd.
410-484-7343

Seven Mile Market
4000 Seven Mile Land
410-653-2000

Shlomo's Kosher Meat
4030 Fallstaff Rd.
410-358-9633

Wasserman & Lemberger Kosher
Meat Market
7006 Reisterstown Rd.
410-486-4191

MASSACHUSETTS

Boston

Anthony Bakery
4 Lake St., Peabody
508-535-5335

Boston Cookie
Framingham Mall, Rte. 30,
Framingham
508-872-1052

Bread Basket Bakery
151 Cochituate Rd., Framingham
508-875-9441

Brick Oven Bakery
237 Ferry St., Malden
617-322-3269

Cheryl Ann's Bakery
1010 W. Roxbury Pkwy.,
Chestnut Hill
617-469-9241

Cookies Express
252 Bussey St., East Dedham
617-461-0044

Donut Shak
487 Westford St., Lowell
508-937-0178

Donuts with a Difference
35 Riverside Ave., Medford
617-396-1021

Dough-C-Donuts
1460 Massachusetts Ave., Arlington
617-643-4550

Fabiano Bakery
7 Somerset Ave., Winthrop
617-846-5946

Green Manor Bakery
31 Tosca Dr., Stoughton
617-828-3018

Lederman's Bakery
1223 Centre St., Newton
617-527-7896

Newman's Bakery
248 Humphrey St., Swampscott
617-592-1550

Ruth's Bake Shop
987 Central St., Stoughton
617-344-8993

Sara's Kitchen
South Shore Plaza, Braintree
617-843-8803

Taam Tov Bakery
305A Harvard St., Brookline
617-566-8136

Tabrizi Bakery
56A Mt. Auburn St., Watertown
617-926-0880

Tuler's Bakery
551 Commonwealth Ave.,
Newton
617-964-5653

Zeppy's Bakery
937 North Main St., Randolph
617-963-9837

MICHIGAN

Detroit

Lakewood Market
Greenfield Rd., Oak Park

MISSOURI

Kansas City

New York Bakery & Delicatessen
7016 Troost St.
816-523-0432

Price Chopper
1030 W. 103rd St.
816-942-4200

St. Louis

Diamant's Market
618 North & South Rd.
314-721-9624

Dierberg's Bakery
Craig Rd.
314-432-8823

Olive & Spoode
314-567-3838
Overland Plaza
314-426-3800

Schnucks Markets Bakeries
Landue Crossing
314-725-7574
Olive & Mason
314-434-7323

Simon Kohn's Kosher Meat Market
& Grocery
10424 Old Olive St. Rd.
314-569-0727

Sol's Kosher Market
8627 Olive St. Rd.
314-993-9977

NEW JERSEY

Atlantic County

Isadore's Kosher Market & Deli
1324 Tilton Rd., Worthfield
(Atlantic City area)
609-383-3635

Bergen County

Ben David Food Emporium
24-28 Fair Lawn Ave., Fair Lawn
201-794-7740

Butterflake Bake Shop
448 Cedar Ln., Teaneck
201-836-3516

Carousel Chocolates
1117 Trafalgar St., Teaneck
201-836-3306

Chopstix
172 W. Englewood Ave., Teaneck
201-833-0200

David's Fresh Fish Market
736 Chestnut Ave., Teaneck
201-928-0888

Fancy Delights
492A Cedar Ln., Teaneck
201-487-4035

Glatt Express Market
1400 Queen Anne Rd., Teaneck
201-837-8110

Glatt World Market
89 Newbridge Rd., Bergenfield
201-439-9675

Gruenbaum Bakeries
477B Cedar Ln., Teaneck
201-836-3516

Kosher by the Case & Less
255 Van Nostrand Ave.,
Englewood
201-568-2281

Kosher Express
22-16 Morlot Ave., Fair Lawn
201-791-8818

Ma'adan
446 Cedar Ln., Teaneck
201-692-0192

The Menageries
41 E. Palisade Ave., Englewood
201-569-2704

New Royal Bake Shop
19-09 Fair Lawn Ave., Fair Lawn
201-796-6565

Petak's Glatt Kosher Fine Foods
19-03 Fair Lawn Ave., Fair Lawn
201-797-5010

Radburn Cake Box
24-04 Fair Lawn Ave., Fair Lawn
201-796-3800

Royal Too Bakery
19-09 Fair Lawn Ave., Fair Lawn
201-796-6565

Teaneck Glatt
409 Cedar Lane
Teaneck
201-692-0092

Essex County

Zayda's
309 Irvington Ave., South Orange

Passaic County

Kosher Hot Bagel & Bialys
237 Main Ave., Passaic
201-472-1244†

NEW YORK

Bronx

Glatt Emporium
3711 Riverdale Ave.
718-884-1200

Glatt Shop
3450 Johnson Ave.
718-548-4855

Gruenebaum's Bakery
3550 Johnson Ave.
718-884-5656

Heislers Pastry Shop
3700 Riverdale Ave.
718-549-0770

Nathan's Kosher Meat Market
570 W. 235th St.
718-548-1723

---

†As of June 1, 1997, the area code
for this number will be 973.

Rolen Bagels
3601 Riverdale Ave.
718-884-9555

Second Helping Glatt Kosher Food
3532 Johnson Ave.
718-548-1818

Brooklyn

Cheese Plus Things
1117 Ave. J
718-377-4911

Dave's Kosher Meat Mart
3604 Nostrand Ave.
718-648-8500

Flaum Appetizers
40 Lee Ave.
718-387-7934

Glatt Butcher
5704 New Utrecht Ave.
718-435-5243

Glatt Mart
1205 Ave. M
718-338-4040
The only kosher butcher in the city
that prepares kosher buffalo meat

Glatt Pack Kosher Meat
4815 13th Ave.
718-633-6346

Glick Brothers
448 Ave. P
718-645-5254
3719 Nostrand Ave.
718-769-7705
520 Neptune Ave.
718-372-9394

Grodko Kosher Butcher Shop
8402 20th Ave.
718-449-2924

I & D Glatt
482 Ave. P
718-339-8555

Israel Glatt
4907 13th Ave.
718-436-2948

Jerusalem Glatt Meats
710 Kings Hwy.
718-376-7443

Jerusalem Kosher Meat Market
4516 Ft. Hamilton Pkwy.
718-633-5555

Joey Glatt Kosher
936 Kings Hwy.
718-382-2527

Korn's Kosher Bread Basket
4309 13th Ave.
718-435-2852

Kosher French Baguette
683 MacDonald Ave.
718-633-4994

Kosher Korner
492 Kings Hwy.
718-375-3442
Specializes in Middle Eastern
foods

Kosherland
1536 Coney Island Ave.
718-338-9346

Kosher Meat Farm
2104 Ralph Ave.
718-531-7250

Kosher Plaza Supermarket
1223 Coney Island Ave.
718-252-8555

Landau's Supermarket
4510 18th Ave.
718-633-0633

Lee Avenue Kosher Bakery
73 Lee Ave.
718-387-4736

Mehadrin Supermarket
5124 12th Ave.
718-435-2678

Mendy's Supermarket
2213 65th St.
718-837-0782

Nadler's Kosher Meats
613 Brighton Beach Ave.
718-648-6900

Pasternack Kosher Butcher
422 Ditmars Ave.
718-438-4411

Pick N Pay
1907 Ave. M
718-377-4050

Presser Kosher Bakery
1720 Ave. M
718-375-5088

R & W Glatt Kosher Butchers
1501 Coney Island Ave.
718-377-7391

Ralph Zaken
3069 W. First St.

Raskin's Fish Market
320 Kingston Ave.
718-756-9521

Rosner Kosher
719 Ave. U
718-645-8486

Strauss Bakery
5209 13th Ave.
718-851-7728

Weiss Homemade Kosher Bakery
5011 13th Ave.
718-438-0407

Weiss Kosher Meat Market
5520 13th Ave.
718-871-5448
1214 Ave. M
718-376-6116

Yerushalayim Famous Bakery
1336 39th St.
718-633-5100

Manhattan

Ben's Cheese Shop
181 E. Houston St.
212-254-8290

David's Kosher Meats
221 E. Broadway
212-964-1232

Feinschmecker Fine Foods
1239 First Ave.
212-794-2365

Fischer Brothers & Leslie Kosher
Meat & Poultry & Take Out
230 W. 72nd St.
212-787-1715

Gertels Bakery
53 Hester St.
212-982-3250

Gisella's Secrets
412 E. 9th St.
212-777-0695
Kosher sugarless, salt-free bakery

Grossinger's Uptown Bakery
570 Columbus Ave.
212-874-6996

Gus's Pickles
35 Essex St.
212-254-4477

H&H Bagel
2239 Broadway
212-595-8000

Leibel's Kosher Specialities
39 Essex St.
212-254-0335

Long Island Glatt Kosher Meat &
Poultry
829 W. 181st St.
212-795-0248

Miller's Cheese & Appetizing
2192 Broadway
212-496-8855

Moishe's Home Made Kosher
Bakery
181 E. Houston St.
212-475-9624
115 Second Ave.
212-505-8555

Murray's House of Prime Kosher
Meat
507 Grand St.
212-254-0180

Park East Kosher Butcher
1163 Madison Ave.
212-737-9800

Royale Kosher Bakery shop
237 W. 72nd St.
212-874-5642

Stern's Glatt Kosher Emporium
526 Amsterdam Ave.
212-875-1731

Zabar's Food Shop
2245 Broadway
212-787-2000
Wide selection of kosher foods,
delicacies; also sells nonkosher
foods

Queens

Aaron's Gourmet Emporium
63-36 Woodhaven Blvd., Rego Park
718-205-1992

Aaron's Kosher Meats
156-15 Aguilar Ave., Flushing
718-380-8209

Abe's Glatt Kosher Meats
98-106 Queens Blvd., Forest Hills
718-459-5820

Akboch Kosher Meat Market
98-54 63rd Rd., Rego Park
718-896-7276

Block & Faulk Meats
112-06 Queens Blvd., Forest Hills
718-261-7463

Brach's Glatt Self Service Meat &
Supermarket
72-49 Main St., Kew Gardens Hills
718-544-7448

Burkho Meat Store
65-49 99th St., Rego Park
718-459-8480

Chai Kosher
64-37 108th St., Forest Hills
718-897-9619

D&W Kosher Meats
61-42 Springfield Ave., Bayside
718-225-1550

Edal's Kosher Meat & Poultry
79-09 Main St., Kew Gardens
718-380-1366

Finest Kosher Meats & Poultry
63-71 108th St., Forest Hills
718-897-3053

G&I Kosher Bakeries
69-40 Main St., Kew Gardens Hills
800-326-1155, 718-261-1155
72-22 Main St., Kew Gardens Hills
718-544-8736

G&K Kosher Meat & Poultry
115-06 Rockaway Beach Blvd.,
Rockaway Park
718-474-6704

Gotta Getta Bagel
107-09 Continental Ave., Forest
Hills
718-793-1640

Herman Glick & Sons Glatt Kosher
Food Emporium
100-15 Queens Blvd., Forest Hills
718-896-7736

Hershkowitz Glatt Kosher
164-08 69th Ave., Flushing
718-591-0750

Jay Dee Kosher Bakery
98-92 Queens Blvd.
Forest Hills
718-459-5365

Kosher Bagels & Bialys
147-23 Union Tpke.
Fresh Meadows
718-591-3356

Lazar's Kosher Meats
100-30 Queens Blvd., Forest Hills
718-897-6635

Main Street Bagels & Appetizing
72-26 Main St., Kew Gardens Hills
718-793-8100

Mazurs Market Place
254-51 Horace Harding Blvd.,
Little Neck
718-428-5000

Piquanty Grocery
68-29 Main St.
Kew Garden Hills
718-575-1587

Queens Pita Bakery
68-38 Main St., Kew Gardens Hills
718-263-8000

Simcha Kosher Meats
138-40 86th Ave., Jamaica
718-206-4861

Super Glatt
189-23 Union Tpke.,
Fresh Meadows
718-776-7727

Supersol Kosher Supermarket
68-18 Main St., Kew Gardens Hills
718-268-6469

Tikvah Kosher Meat Mart
105-45 64th Rd., Forest Hills
718-896-8515

Union Turnpike Meat Corp.
179-14 Union Tpke.,
Fresh Meadows
718-969-4322

Staten Island

Famous Kosher Bakery
2208 Victory Blvd.
718-494-1411

Kosher Island Glatt Kosher Take
Home Foods
2206 Victory Blvd.
718-698-5800

Triple Glatt
446 Nome Ave.
718-982-6400

Long Island

Aderet Kosher Food Market
726 Old Bethpage Rd.,
Old Bethpage
516-293-3144

Cohen's Kosher Meat & Poultry
1330 Broadway, Hewlett
516-374-1129

Commack Kosher Meats & Catering
132 E. Jericho Tpke., Commack
516-543-2300

Country Boy Bakery
256 East Park Ave., Long Beach
516-889-7295

Elat Prime Meats
497 N. Middle Neck Rd.,
Great Neck
516-829-8181

Emmet Kosher Meat Market
713 Middle Neck Rd., Great Neck
516-829-5454

Five Towns Kosher
1324 Peninsula Rd., Hewlett
516-791-9877

G&I Bakery
536 Central Ave., Cedarhurst
516-374-2525

Glatt Palace
22 East Park Ave., Long Beach
516-897-9250

Gourmet Glatt Emporium
137-139 Spruce St., Cedarhurst
516-569-2662

Greenfield's Foodtown
1054 Old Country Rd., Plainview
516-938-2250
444 Woodbury Rd., Plainview
516-938-0240

Jericho Kosher Meat Market
441 N. Broadway, Jericho
516-938-7900

Kosher Emporium
1984 Merrick Rd., Merrick
516-378-6463

Kosher Meat Farm
1172 Wantagh Ave., Wantagh
516-781-6296

Lawrence Kosher Meat Market
330 Central Ave., Lawrence
516-569-3683

Long Island Kosher Meats
1984 Merrick Blvd., Merrick
516-379-4263

Max's Appetizing & Deli
1016 Broadway, Woodmere
516-374-0617

Nassau Kosher Meats & Catering
495 Bellmore Ave., East Meadow
516-333-1616

New Hyde Park Kosher Meats
1620 Marcus Ave., New Hyde Park
516-488-3396

Pearl's Kosher Bake Shop
26 Manetto Hills Rd., Plainview
516-935-5225

Plainview Kosher Meats
1113 Old Country Rd., Plainview
516-681-4418

Roslyn Kosher Foods
1044 Willis Ave., Albertson
516-621-9615

Shop Glatt Mart
172 E. Park Ave., Long Beach
516-897-8657

Supersol Kosher Supermarket
330 Central Ave., Lawrence
516-295-3300

Woodbury Kosher Meat
428 S. Oyster Bay Rd., Hicksville
516-681-7766

Zomick's Bakery
444 Central Ave., Cedarhurst
516-569-5520

Rockland County

M & S Kosher
191 S. Main Street
New City

Village Kosher Meat Market
303A North Main, Spring Valley
914-356-0241

Westchester County

Centuck Kosher Meat Market
662 Tuckahoe Rd., Yonkers
914-779-3683

Heisler's Pastry
1321 North Ave., New Rochelle
914-235-8201

Sammy's Kosher Meat Market
720 Bedford Rd., Bedford Hills
914-241-4477

Scarsdale Kosher Emporium
1066 Willmot Rd., Scarsdale
914-472-2240

Syon Kosher Meats
 2558 Central Park Ave., Yonkers
914-779-8100

OHIO

Cincinnati

Marx Hot Bagels
7617 Reading Rd., Cincinnati
3616 Northland Blvd., Springdale

Cleveland

Altman Quality Kosher Meat
Market
2185 S. Green Rd.
216-381-7615

Boris Kosher Meats
14406 Cedar Rd.
216-382-5330

Lax & Mandel Bakery
2070 S. Taylor Rd.,
Cleveland Heights
216-932-6445

Unger's Kosher Bakery & Food
Shop
1831 S. Taylor Rd.
216-321-7176

Columbus

Bexley Kosher Market
3012 E. Broad St.
614-231-3653

Martin's Kosher Foods
3685 E. Broad St.
614-213-3653

Marx Hot Bagels
9701 Kenwood Rd., Blue Ash

Sammy's N.Y. Bagel & Deli
40 North James Rd.
614-237-2444

OREGON

Portland

Albertson's Meat Market
5414 SW Beaverton-Hillsdale Hwy.
503-246-1713

Portland Bagel Bakery
3575 NW Yeon St.
503-228-4975

Ron's Center Deli
6651 SW Capitol Hwy.
503-244-0664

PENNSYLVANIA

Northampton County

Buy the Dozen Bakery
219 Haverford Ave., Nazareth
610-667-9440

Philadelphia

Bestcake Bakery
1594 Haverford Ave.
215-878-1127

Liss Bakery
215-474-8550

Pittsburgh

Kosher Mart
2121 Murray Ave.
412-421-4450

Pastries Unlimited
2119 Murray Ave.
412-521-6323

Prime Kosher
1916 Murray Ave.
412-421-1015

TENNESSEE

Memphis

Carls Bakery
1688 Jackson Ave.
901-276-2304

Rubenstein's Deli & Fine Kosher
Food
4965 Summer Ave.
901-682-3801

TEXAS

Dallas

Tom Thumb Bakery & Deli
11920 Preston Rd., Preston Forest
Shopping Center
214-392-2501

Houston

Ashcraft Bakery
1301 North First, Bellaire
713-666-2163

Kroger Supermarket Bakery
S. Post Oak & West Bellfort
713-721-7691

Le Moulin European Bakery
5645 Beechnut
713-799-1618

New York Bagels
9724 Hillcroft
713-723-5879

Simon's Gourmet Kosher Foods
5411 S. Braeswood
713-729-5333

Three Brothers Bakery
4036 S. Braeswood
713-666-2551

WASHINGTON

Seattle

Albertson's Food & Drug Store
Chain
Several locations

Bagel Deli
340 15th E.
206-322-2471
Bagels, bialys, brownies

Dunkin Donuts
2921 Martin Luther King Way S.
206-722-9247

Mishpochen Rye Company
5028 Wilson Ave. S.
206-725-1920
Bakery

Noah's Grocery
4700 50th St.
206-725-4267

Puget Consumers Co-op Natural
Markets
Several locations
206-723-2720

Varon's Kosher Meats
3931 Martin Luther King Way S.
206-723-0240

CANADA

Halifax, Nova Scotia

IGA Supermarket
Quinpaol St.
902-425-1498
Kosher meats, cheeses

Stone Hearth Bakery
Argyle St.
902-425-7752

Toronto, Ontario

Akwa's Kosher Foods
3858 Bathurst St.
416-635-0470

Kosher and Natural Foods
3413 Bathurst St.
416-789-7174

My Zaidy's Bakery
7241 Bathurst St., Thornhill
905-731-3831

Yossi's Fine Foods
4117 Bathurst St.
416-635-9509

Vancouver, British Columbia

Sabra Bakery & Grocery
3844 Oak St.
604-733-4912

Winnipeg, Manitoba

Bathurst Market
204-338-4911

Omnitsky's Meat Market
1428 Main St.
204-586-8271

OTHER RESOURCES FOR THE KOSHER CONSUMER

B'nai B'rith Hillel Foundation
1640 Rhode Island Ave. NW
Washington, DC 20036
Compiles the *Hillel Guide to Jewish Life on Campus*, published by The Princeton Review, paperback, $17. It includes information on colleges and universities that have kosher dining arrangements for their students.

The Jewish Homemaker Magazine
420 Lincoln Rd., Ste. 409, Miami Beach, FL 33139
800-237-2304, 305-673-3530
Bimonthly publication that incorporates *The Kosher Food Guide* of the OK Laboratories. $11.97 one year, $19.97 two years, $26.97 three years.

Kashrus: The Magazine for the Kosher Consumer
P.O. Box 204, Brooklyn, NY 11204
800-825-0061, 718-336-8544
Five issues a year. Subscription $18.00 one year, $33 two years, $45 three years, $60 four years.

KosherMall
http://www.koshermall.com
Kosher recipes, information on how to kasher everything from ovens to silverware, information on kosher products and certifying agencies

INDEX